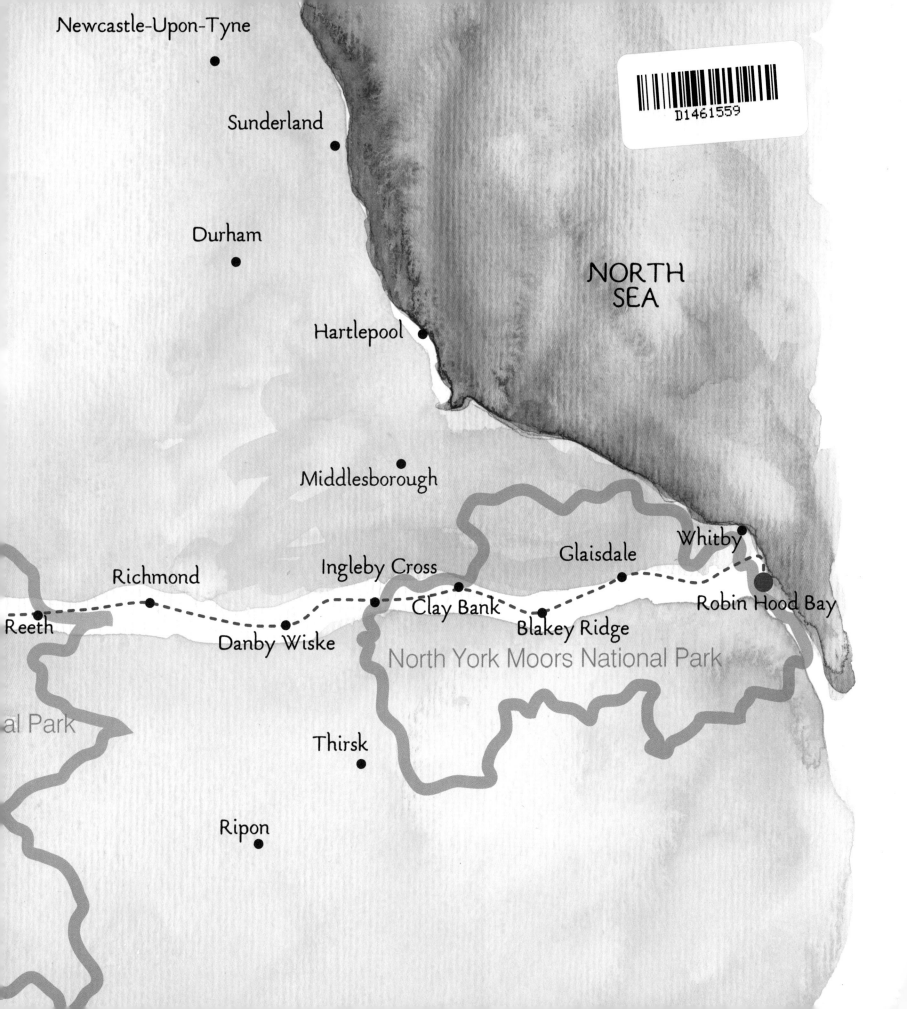

Newcastle-Upon-Tyne

Sunderland

Durham

Hartlepool

NORTH
SEA

Middlesborough

Richmond

Ingleby Cross

Glaisdale

Whitby

Reeth

Clay Bank

Robin Hood Bay

Danby Wiske

Blakey Ridge

North York Moors National Park

al Park

Thirsk

Ripon

THE COAST TO COAST WALK KAREN FRENKEL

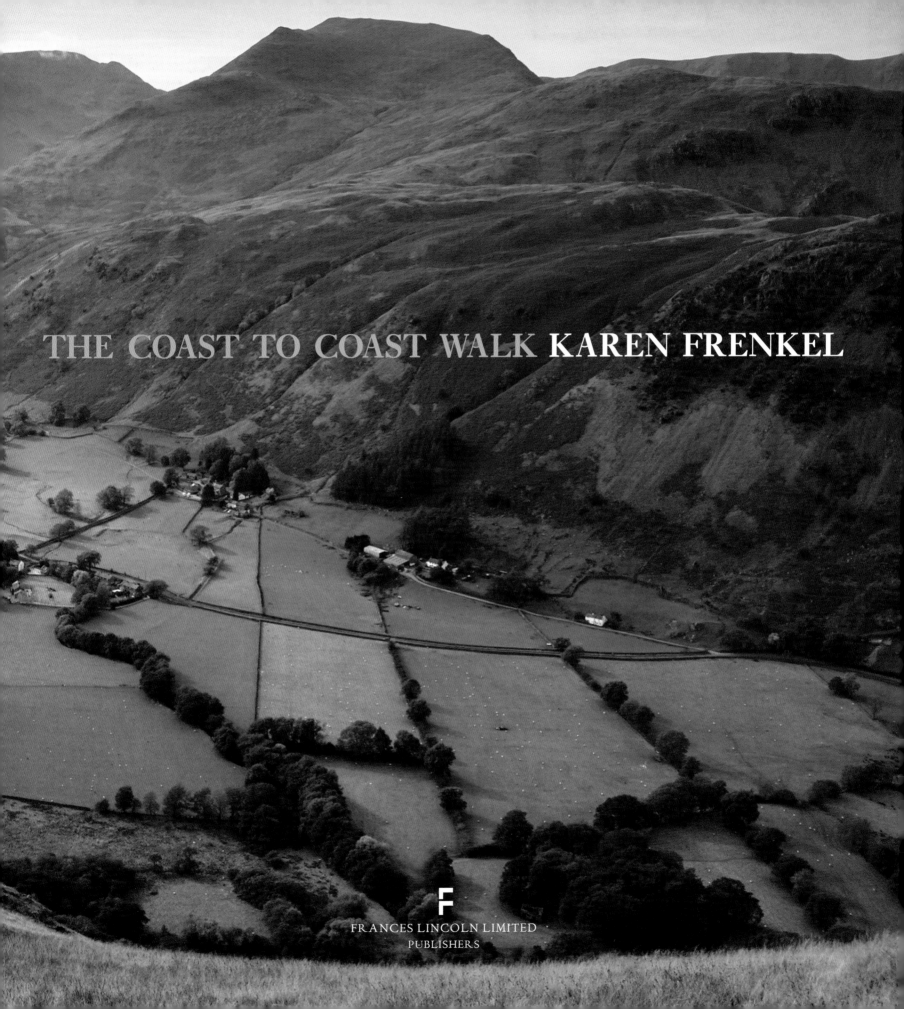

THE COAST TO COAST WALK KAREN FRENKEL

F

FRANCES LINCOLN LIMITED
PUBLISHERS

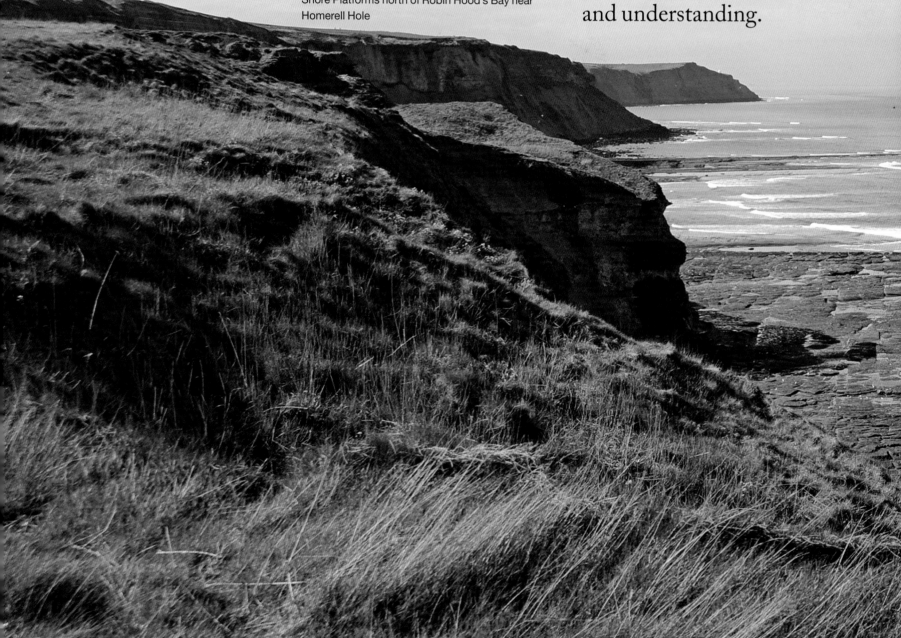

Frances Lincoln Limited
4 Torriano Mews
Torriano Avenue
London NW5 2RZ
www.franceslincoln.com

A catalogue record for this book is available
from the British Library.

ISBN 978-0-7112-3217-4

Printed and bound in China

1 2 3 4 5 6 7 8 9

PAGE 1
Top Angle Tarn in winter
Bottom Views from Satura Crag towards
Martindale Common

PAGE 2-3
Looking over Patterdale Valley into Deepdale

PAGE 4-5
Shore Platforms north of Robin Hood's Bay near
Homerell Hole

DEDICATION

To David, for his remarkable
support, patience and
packhorse duties, and to
my friends and family,
who have been so helpful
and understanding.

CONTENTS

6   Introduction

10   Through the Lake District

38   Into the Vale of Eden

54   Across the Yorkshire Dales

82   The Vale of Mowbray

94   The North York Moors

110   Recommended Reading
Photographer's Notes

111   Acknowledgements

112   Index

Introduction

History of the route

Alfred Wainwright's great idea of a walk from west to east across the north of England, linking St Bees on the Irish Sea to Robin Hood's Bay on the North Sea, was first published in 1973. The route crosses three of the most spectacular national parks in the country, taking in some of northern England's most dramatic and beautiful landscapes.

Not only is it pretty direct but it sustains an amazing level of interest and variety throughout its length. There are no sections that can be said to be tedious, apart from when an over-optimistic schedule or perhaps seriously bad weather results in mental or physical fatigue. Road walking is kept to a minimum, and the footpaths and bridleways bring a string of constant pleasant surprises, often well off the normal car-based tourist routes.

The route was obviously the result of many years of painstaking research and hard footwork. Admittedly, in his first edition Wainwright made a few mistakes about access and upset a few landowners. Subsequent editions published by Frances Lincoln have been revised and corrected to prevent trespass, and doubtless further changes will be made as more and more people from across the world take on Wainwright's challenge, putting pressures on the route that would have horrified him.

The route in brief

Wainwright's route is 190 miles long, travelling from the red sandstone cliffs of St Bees on the Cumbrian coast. It threads through the spectacular igneous and glaciated rocky landscape of the Lake District National Park with its majestic mountains, fells, lakes, rivers and tarns to Shap. It then enters limestone country and crosses the less well known but lovely, verdant and peaceful Eden Valley to Kirkby Stephen.

From here it climbs up to the watershed of Northern England near Nine Standards Rigg. Here the 'big sky' country of the limestone Yorkshire Dales National Park begins and runs through Swaledale, one of the most beautiful dales, to the historic town of Richmond.

LEFT Ullswater at sunset

TOP View over Ennerdale from Pillar Ridge towards Fleetwith Pike

From here the terrain is flat, but pleasantly gentle, quiet and agricultural as the route crosses the fertile Vale of Mowbray through to Ingleby Cross. Finally, there is a climb up into the Cleveland Hills. The last section crosses the heather-clad North York Moors National Park until it skirts the limestone, sandstone and shale North Sea cliffs to its goal, the quaint little fishing village of Robin Hood's Bay, which clings to the steep hillside and is full of enticing treats for weary walkers. But only after they have followed the tradition of dipping their toes in the North Sea.

About this book

This book is not a route guide but a celebration of the spectacular landscape encountered along the way. It is a book to ponder over and will hopefully encourage people to return and check out those places they have missed or did not have time to visit.

As a child I loved to visit the Lake District. It was my spiritual home, and I took many camping trips throughout the year there. Unknown to me then, the Coast to Coast route passed right by one of my favourite camp sites near Stonethwaite. Later, I was lucky enough to live for a while on the edge of the Yorkshire Dales, and it was then that I fell in love with the area around Swaledale.

I heard about this walk and for many years it remained on my list of things to do, as it ran so close to many places which were special to me. When I left a career in chemistry in 1996 to become a professional landscape photographer, it made sense to me that one day it would be a wonderful project to catalogue the landscapes encountered along the route, throughout the seasons in different light and weather conditions. After all, I had unknowingly photographed parts of the route over the years. In 2009 my proposal to Frances Lincoln was accepted and my adventure to photograph this route in earnest began.

In order to do the landscape justice, it had to be photographed throughout the year, targeting the different regions when I felt the scenery would be at its best. With the broad geological differences across the region, the landscape varies in appearance depending on the seasons.

For example, I targeted the North York Moors when

they were a purple haze of heather in August and September. The Lake District is beautiful in autumn when the bracken-clad mountain slopes, sedges and mixed deciduous woodlands are an explosion of colour and the boulder-strewn streams become torrents. The Yorkshire Dales peak in June and July when the hay meadows are full of wild flowers, and the Vale of Mowbray is colourful with pink cherry blossom, swathes of hedgerow flowers and the fields of oilseed rape appear as a luminous yellow carpet as they spread across the landscape in April and May.

There are certain weather conditions such as clear, stormy light, frost and snow, or during an amazing pink sunrise or sunset, when any landscape can look spectacular. However much planning goes into a shoot, an element of luck is sometimes needed to be in the right place at the right time to capture special images.

It is for the above reasons, together with the practicalities of carrying heavy camera gear and spending hours (or sometimes days) on one section in order to optimise the light, that I have not walked the route continuously. If I had, it is unlikely that every day would have given me beautiful images with perfect

LEFT Drumlins in Deepdale

ABOVE Patterdale

The layout

I have split the book into the five areas: The Lake District, The Vale of Eden, The Yorkshire Dales, The Vale of Mowbray and the North York Moors. At the beginning of each section, a short introduction outlines the key features of that area, with points of interest along the route, together with how its appearance changes through the seasons.

For each of the images there are extended captions which outline a little about the area or may include stories associated with the pictures. I've noted the time of year the pictures were taken to enable people to compare these with when they may have walked that section and as an indicator of how that scene looks at that particular time. Also, as I met so many wonderful people and tried to include a few willing models in the images, they may remember me if they eventually get to see this book.

For those interested in photography, at the end of the book is a brief chapter on how the photographs were taken, the equipment used and any problems encountered. There is also an index of places and subjects photographed, cross-referenced to the page numbers.

light, and the book would not have had the variety throughout its pages if taken in the same season. After immersing myself for days at a time in the different areas, I occasionally also found things slightly off-route that I thought should be included.

It became obvious to me that this route should not be rushed. Admittedly, many people have a limited time to do it and need to push on in order to complete the walk in two weeks. However, for those who have the luxury of more time, the scenery is so spectacular that it is worth fitting in those extra days in order to explore the areas in more detail. Many do the walk in stages, and from my own experience, people should consider trying the walk at different times of year to witness the way it changes with the seasons. This would also spread the load of visitors and make accommodation booking a little easier.

From a chance conversation I had with a Coast to Coaster in Patterdale YHA, I have tried to avoid too many chocolate box views taken in brilliant weather. We were discussing the book and he was adamant that I should show the route as many people really experienced it, i.e. in stormy, wet, dull, misty and damp weather at times. I made note of this and have tried to include more typical scenes on inclement days.

In conclusion

Having completed the book, there is just one thing left for me to do. Apart from constantly returning to some of my favourite places along the route at different times to improve upon these images, I now need to take up the challenge and become a proper Coast to Coaster and complete the walk in one go.

No doubt I'll still take my camera but will have to restrict the rest of the gear to a sensible amount. I'll not be able to linger around too long waiting for the light and I'm probably not fit enough, but I'm determined to have a go. I look forward to meeting the great variety of people who do this route, only this time I'll be one of them and not some recluse who has to sacrifice the pub at the end of the day in order to stand alone on a hillside for hours waiting for the light and missing out on the chat, good food and drink. I can't wait.

Through the Lake District

St Bees to Shap
100.6km /62.5 miles

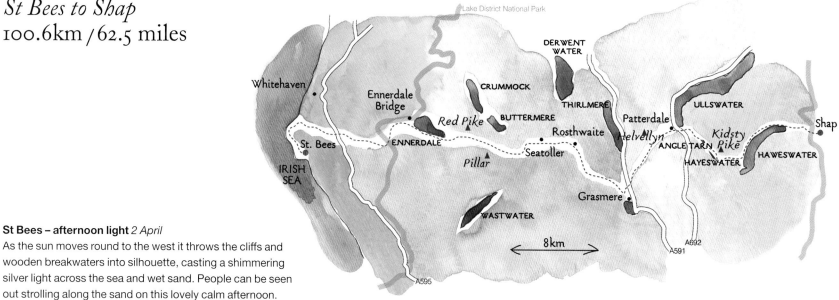

St Bees – afternoon light *2 April*
As the sun moves round to the west it throws the cliffs and wooden breakwaters into silhouette, casting a shimmering silver light across the sea and wet sand. People can be seen out strolling along the sand on this lovely calm afternoon.

The route begins with a walk along the spectacular red sandstone cliffs around St Bees Head. In spring and summer, the cliffs are alive with nesting seabirds and coastal plants cling to the rocky ledges, creating miniature rock gardens. Yellow gorse flanks much of the route, adding another dimension to the senses with its strong scent of coconut.

Heading inland between Sandwith and Cleator, flower-decked lanes make pleasant walking before the first leg-warming hill of Dent has to be climbed. From here, there are magnificent views and the fells of Lakeland beckon. One last treat before Ennerdale is the quiet valley of Uldale and Nannycatch Beck, which is reached after a very steep descent from this rounded fell.

Nearing Ennerdale Bridge, views into the jaws of Ennerdale open up and we enter one of the remotest and least visited valleys in the Lakes. The route follows the southern shore of Ennerdale Lake before crossing the River Liza and then runs alongside it into the coniferous depths of Ennerdale Forest. It is not until you emerge from the forest near the Black Sail youth hostel that the landscape opens out and the wilder Lakeland mountain scenery is experienced, as the slopes of Brandreth and Grey Knotts are ascended. Once height is gained, it is tempting to explore other lofty peaks in the area such as High Stile and Red Pike, before descending to the green slate quarries of the Honister Pass.

This section through the heart of the Lake District

near to England's highest peaks is spectacular in all seasons and weather conditions. The mountains bring fast-changing weather and therefore, ever changing light. In winter, the tops can be covered in snow, tarns and lakes become frozen and shadows are long. The low sun sculpts out every feature in the terrain, casting a warm glow over the burnished bracken-clad fells, scattered with rocky outcrops. The layers of rock were shifted and shaped by folding and uplifting and then scoured by glaciers and meltwater to form the distinctive topography of today's Lake District, with its smooth, U-shaped valleys like Buttermere, Borrowdale or Grisedale and steep-sided ridges such as Striding Edge on Helvellyn, all examples which we will see along the route.

The highest and craggiest mountains of the central Lake District are made up of the Borrowdale Volcanics, very hard lavas and ashes formed from eruptions about 450 million years ago. Borrowdale is landscape perfection, a fertile valley surrounded by rugged mountains, flanked by native deciduous woodland and, courtesy of the highest rainfall levels in England, dissected by clear, sparkling, rocky streams.

A climb out of the valley onto wilder fells near Greenup Edge is soon rewarded by the descent to sylvan Grasmere, once the home of Lakeland poet William Wordsworth. In spring, Wordworth's daffodils still nod their heads and the tranquil lake reflects the surrounding fells.

The majesty of this mountain scenery is sustained all the way over to Patterdale near Ullswater and then up past lonely Angle Tarn to the route's highest point of Kidsty Pike near High Street. On a route once frequented by marching

Sellafield at sunset *12 April*
The hustle and bustle of the beach are soon left behind and a lovely peaceful cliff top walk is disturbed only by the sounds of wheeling seabirds. While waiting for the light earlier in the morning, I met a couple setting out for the North Sea even though they had done the walk several times before. They loved it so much. As you climb slightly higher, Sellafield nuclear power station comes into full view. Although controversial, it provides major employment in this less touristy part of West Cumbria. The foreground gorse and sandstone cliffs take on a rich, warm tone in the setting sun.

Roman legionaries, the crowds disappear as the route descends from this remote spot above Riggindale down to the wilder shores of Haweswater Reservoir. Here a lonely golden eagle soars and, during the rutting season in October, red deer can be heard bellowing across the water, beneath which lies the flooded remains of the village of Mardale.

Finally, the route flattens out as it meanders by rivers and streams through the Lowther Valley in pleasant rolling scenery. This area from Riggindale is said to have inspired JRR Tolkein when writing *The Lord of the Rings*. Here limestone scenery starts to creep in as the path passes the monastic ruins of Shap Abbey, leaving the national park before reaching the village of Shap on the A6, now quiet thanks to the M6 motorway which runs parallel to it and which has relieved it of much of the traffic to and from Scotland.

Coastal path in morning light *13 April*
Morning sunshine illuminates the fabulous cliffs of St Bees Head beyond Fleswick Bay. Fleswick is a natural gash in the cliffs and the route descends steeply down before climbing back up to North Head. On the top of North Head is St Bees lighthouse, which is now used for holiday accommodation.

St Bees

The name St Bees is thought to originate from St Bega, the daughter of an Irish King who, according to legend, in AD 650 fled across the Irish Sea in the company of nuns to seek peace and solitude. Her ship was wrecked on rocks near Whitehaven. Travelling south, she found a quiet, suitable spot here and was given permission by the landowner to settle, eventually establishing a nunnery on the site of the church. Nearby St Bees Head is the most westerly point of northern England, which probably brought it to the attention of Alfred Wainwright when first plotting his great excursion.

Before the start of the walk, it is customary to dip your boots into the Irish Sea. Waiting until high tide clearly doesn't significantly shorten the walk, so I lingered around St Bees for a whole day and took a few pictures before the steep ascent onto the RSPB nature reserve of South Head, and the start of the adventure to Robin Hood's Bay.

Fleswick Bay

A small diversion down to the bay before the steep ascent to St. Bees Head is well worth the effort. The dramatic red sandstone sea cliffs are full of surprising rock formations and hanging gardens in the rock crevices, with caves and fantastically-coloured pebbles on the beach below.

ABOVE Looking out to sea from under a rock shelter *13 April*
This made a fantastic lunch spot, looking at the cloud formations reflected on the sea and patches of sunlight dancing on the water. An incredibly weathered, dimpled red sandstone boulder made a great foreground.

RIGHT Nesting kittiwakes on the sea cliffs around St Bees Head
13 April
North of Fleswick Bay, the RSPB has constructed some little viewing platforms in order to observe the large variety of sea birds which can be seeing both nesting and wheeling around the cliffs. They include cormorants, gannets, kittiwakes, black guillemots, guillemots, razorbills, fulmars, black-backed and herring gulls, and puffins. Here kittiwakes cling precariously to the rocky ledges. There were so many nesting birds their droppings had turned the cliffs white in places.

LEFT CENTRE Colourful pebbles on the beach
13 April
On closer inspection, the pebbles on the beach are not just red sandstone but different coloured granites as well.

LEFT Rock garden *13 April*
Common scurvy grass on this damp, rocky ledge makes a perfect rock garden.

Sunset over the Isle of Man *12 April*
At the end of a hazy day, Goat Fell on the Isle of Man looms out of the
distance, 50km/30 miles away. It was the first glimpse I'd had of it all
day, looking splendidly pink as the sun dropped below the horizon,
and a fine sight as I said goodbye to the sea and turned inland.

Stile over a deer fence on Dent Fell *14 April*
Although only a modest 352m/1,155ft high, Dent Fell and this enormous stile are good warm ups in preparation for the mountains of the Lakes. However, the views from the top are magnificent and well worth the effort, stretching as far as the Solway Firth and the Isle of Man.

Views over Nannycatch *14 April*

From the top, the path makes an incredibly steep, knee-wrenching descent down into Uldale and Nannycatch. There are lovely views over Uldale towards Sillathwaite and Blakeley Raise, the boundary of the Lake District National Park. This is a quiet, little-known area of the Lakes, and I vowed to return one day and explore more thoroughly.

Nannycatch Gate *14 April*

Sheltered from the wind, and under the boughs of two lovely trees, this is a great place for a snack stop, as Nannycatch Beck trickles along under Raven Crag. It is actually a place where three steep valleys meet and their becks converge. After a dry spell, the little footbridge was hardly needed, one jump would suffice.

TOP Views towards Ennerdale from Lanefoot *14 April*
As you descend the fell road into Ennerdale Bridge, views open up into the jaws of Ennerdale. In spring, the fields are full of lambs playing against a backdrop of the Coast to Coast's first high Lakeland fells. The lake is hidden, but the sharp pimple of Red Pike and cloud-topped High Stile can clearly be seen rising above Ennerdale Forest.

ABOVE Views across Ennerdale Lake towards Pillar Ridge from the northern shore *14 April*
This view in early spring across the blue water, and beyond to the dark crags of Bowness Knott, shows Pillar dominating the ridge in the distance. From this angle, Pillar Rock, which is a challenge for rock climbers, can clearly be seen on its left hand side.

TOP Route up Ennerdale past Black Sail *15 May*

If you don't go up over Pillar Ridge but take the route through Ennerdale Forest, the track emerges from its depths into more wilderness, dominated by Great Gable at the head of the valley. Black Sail youth hostel looks just a tiny speck behind a small clump of trees on the left. Thankfully, Ennerdale forest is changing. The dense conifer plantations, devoid of light and wildlife, are slowly being replaced thanks to the Wild Ennerdale project. Over the last few years, many organisations and individuals have become involved to help save this valley and return it to a more natural state. Wainwright would be proud of them.

ABOVE View down to Crummock Water out to the Irish Sea from Red Pike summit *15 May*

Red Pike is a tough, steep ascent, whether it be from Ennerdale or Buttermere. I remember it only too well in my teens as the place where I experienced my first back problem. Struggling up it bent double with a heavy rucksack on a youth hostelling holiday, on arriving at the top I could not straighten up and was in agony. Sadly, my first memory of Black Sail hostel was a painful one. Today, however, my bag was slightly lighter and I was fine. Here, we look north down the length of Crummock Water towards the Vale of Lorton beyond, with the fells of Grassmoor and Whiteless Pike on the right.

Winter dawn over Buttermere *3 February*

After an unusually luxurious evening for me in the Bridge Hotel in Buttermere (the YHA was shut), I had quick access to the shore before breakfast. It had been an extremely cold night (too cold for camping) and the lake was covered in ice. I just caught a watery sun rising over Fleetwith Pike, lending faint peach colours to the sky. The ice prevented reflections and the grass and roots of this solitary tree and surrounding shoreline were covered in a heavy frost.

LEFT Cottages at Seatoller *13 November*
Back on track, the Coast to Coast passes by Seatoller at the foot of the Honister Pass. Here the dappled afternoon light through the tall conifers flanking this old sunken lane makes a lovely foreground, leading the eye to the pretty whitewashed stone cottages beyond. Fiery autumn tints contrast well with the bright green sunlit grass. Most of the cottages in this tiny settlement were built for workers at the nearby Honister slate quarry. Before the quarry opened in 1643 only a farm existed at Seatoller.

BELOW Looking across to Thorneythwaite Fell
13 November
On the track above Seatoller, it is worth strolling on a little keeping your height as there are fantastic views like this one, looking south across to Thorneythwaite Fell and Comb Gill to the foothills of Glaramara and Allen Crags above Seathwaite, famed for being the wettest valley in England. On this fine bright day, the sunlight sparkles and shimmers across this puddle brimming with water from recent heavy rainfall.

BELOW Looking down into Borrowdale Valley and Rosthwaite village *13 November*

Along this small diversion there are lovely views down to Rosthwaite and across Borrowdale. This must be one of the most beautiful valleys in the Lake District, with rugged crags and towering mountains, sparklingly-clear boulder-strewn rivers and streams, and acres of hillsides covered in natural deciduous woodland. Rosthwaite is the largest of the four settlements in Upper Borrowdale and around it are lush green pastures surrounded by wild hillsides covered in golden bracken and autumn-tinted woodland. The River Derwent runs through the valley on its journey west to Derwentwater.

BOTTOM Images from woodland in Borrowdale

Lichen-covered trees, raindrops on mossy boulders and backlit beech leaves all go to make up the wonderful experience of walking through the ancient deciduous woods around Borrowdale.

Backlit beech leaves *19 September*

Raindrops on moss *23 October*

LEFT Views from Castle Crag south towards Honister *15 November*
Although slightly off route, carrying on along the Allerdale Ramble above Seatoller northwards takes you to one of this region's gems, Castle Crag. A short, sharp, scramble up this little crag, full of piles of old slate quarrying debris, reveals spectacular views in all directions. Today was gloomy, and low cloud envelops the mountain tops, but despite this, the view towards Honister was still breathtaking. A riot of autumn colour, it's easy to see why so many famous landscape painters, writers and poets were attracted to this landscape over the years. A week after this picture was taken, Cumbria had its worst flooding in years, this area being particularly badly hit, with roads and bridges washed away.

BELOW Stonethwaite Valley and Eagle Crag *18 November*
Whenever I walk down this valley it feels like I am coming home. From the age of 12, I was brought camping here about four times a year. My memories are of happiness and freedom. Sometimes with my family or sometimes alone, I would roam the surrounding hills and crags with my faithful scruffy mongrel dog, Scamp. Together with my brother and cousins we would play in the river, having stone-throwing contests or any other contest we could think of. The bulk of Eagle Crag with its rocky terraces dominates the valley. At this time of year, the hawthorn bushes are bursting with bright red berries, and a dusting of snow covers the tops around Greenup.

ABOVE Herdwick sheep in Stonethwaite Valley *7 October*
This flock of Herdwick sheep were being driven back up the valley along the Coast to Coast route. Today, Stonethwaite Beck is fairly low, but I have camped by this river when it has been scarily high, with the force of the water moving heavy boulders downstream. On one particular wet night, I awoke to hear tents ripping and people evacuating the site. The morning revealed my trusty Force 10 tent surrounded by water, and the river about to burst its banks. We got out just in time before the valley was cut off.

LEFT Ravines, Langstrath Beck, Smithymire Island *13 November*
This is the point where the two valleys of Greenup and Langstrath meet, and Langstrath Beck joins Stonethwaite Beck at Smithymire Island. It is a beautiful spot where the two rocky streams converge creating cascades and waterfalls. It is worth coming off route slightly to cross the little footbridge over the beck and explore this small paradise. This exact spot is a particularly special place for me. We would always walk up here with the dogs as soon as we had set up camp further downstream and I spent many a happy summer, swimming, having picnics or just lying propped up on a rock listening to the water as it thundered through the narrow, rocky ravines. On closer inspection, the volcanic rocks by the river have fascinating markings, probably from abrasion during the Ice Age. Oak trees cling from crevices hanging over the ravines, with just a few golden leaves remaining. This must be the best time of year for colour here, when the golds and greens of the trees and the aqua blue of the clear water all blend to create a wonderful natural tapestry.

27

Codale Tarn, Grasmere Common *21 September*
I have to confess that I was actually a little off route and slightly
disorientated when I took this picture. We had ventured off the
Greenup route near the top of Far Easedale Gill in order to take a
shortcut and investigate nearby Sergeant Man. For a short while we
convinced ourselves it was Easedale Tarn we could see. The scale
was difficult to judge and our map reading skills were obviously not
up to scratch. It's not disastrous on a clear, calm day like today but
could be a bad decision in poor weather. However, it was a lovely
area to explore and in which to have lunch. Shafts of sunlight broke
through the cloud and shimmered across the water, drawing us like an
oasis across the jumble of tussocks and crags in this wild landscape.
Sergeant Man can be seen just popping over the brow.

Helm Crag ridge shadows *13 November*
Instead of taking the easy route to Grasmere down Easedale Gill,
it is rewarding to do the higher ridge walk between Calf Crag, Gibson
Knott and Helm Crag and take in the wonderful views across the
valley to Fairfield and Helvellyn. On this November afternoon, the
sun has cast shadows of the ridge on the fells around Dunmail Raise,
sculpting out the wrinkles and hollows in this glaciated landscape and
lighting up the ancient stone walls The bracken, golden at this time of
year, adds extra colour, contrasting well with the patches of grass.

Looking up Far Easedale Gill
15 October
The track runs alongside this lovely old, but quite high wall, which obscures the views a little. As I approached Grasmere, I scrambled up onto higher ground to look back up the valley towards the pastures and Sour Milk Gill. The wall snakes away, topped with thick green moss, and the foreground bracken has freshly turned to a lovely orangey gold. The light is soft and diffuse, showing more detail on the distant hillside. A cup of coffee from my flask made it perfect.

Helm Crag from above Grasmere around Silver Howe *14 November*
Although not on route, this view clearly shows the Helm Crag ridge with the precipitous summit crag of The Howitzer (the only Lakeland summit Wainwright claims never to have stood on). Beyond is the pass of Dunmail Raise, through which the road runs to Thirlmere and Keswick.

Grasmere Church *15 October*

Made famous by writers such as Thomas Gray and Wordsworth, who adored it for its sylvan beauty and tranquil lake, Grasmere attracts thousands of visitors each year. Known worldwide as Wordsworth's home and last resting place, in summer its streets are crowded and bustling, somewhat spoiling the tranquillity. I prefer to visit out of season. In October the foliage surrounding the church is spectacular, with the maple trees a riot of autumnal colour.

Dawn, Grasmere Lake *13 September*

A very chilly night produced this lovely pre-dawn mist over Grasmere Lake. Although fairly early at 6.45am, it was nevertheless a race against time to photograph the mist before it dissipated. I'd hoped for more pink colour to appear in the sky, but it never materialised, and had to be content with the slightly cool look and calm reflections instead. Not a great fan of digital manipulation, I didn't clone the jet trails out. Love or loathe them, unlike in Wordsworth's time they are an increasing feature of our skies nowadays.

Grasmere Reflections *13 September*

By 7.40am, the mist had gone. Sunlight is now catching the tops of the fells lighting Helm Crag on the left, and skimming the top of Great Tongue with Tongue Gill still in shadow. If you stopped overnight in Grasmere, there is no reason to rush straight to Patterdale too early at this time of year, unless you're exploring Helvellyn or St. Sunday Crag on the way. In good weather, it's much more pleasant to take your time, have another slice of toast, explore the lakeside and wait for the sun to reach the valley bottom before setting out. Patterdale is only seven miles away and it is a relatively easy day.

BOTTOM Striding Edge, Helvellyn *8 September*

Keen on high mountains, Wainwright recommends the alternative diversion up to Helvellyn, and it is certainly worthwhile if time and energy allows. Here I am looking down from Helvellyn summit (950m/3,118ft) south west onto Striding Edge as the mist begins to clear, with the steep slopes of St Sunday Crag as a backdrop. This famously exposed ridge can get very busy on days of good weather. On close inspection you can see the ridge top dotted with people, sometimes having to queue in order to pass each other.

TOP Helvellyn Ridge from St Sunday Crag *14 September*

As rewarding as Helvellyn and much quieter, the alternative route to Patterdale from Grisedale Tarn traverses up to St Sunday Crag, along the ridge and then down into Patterdale. Not only are there great views to Helvellyn on the way up to the ridge, but fantastic views all around once on the summit. This view looks straight across over Grisedale Valley to Nethermost Cove and Striding Edge. My sheep models are not the local hardy Herdwick breed, but appear to be freshly-sheared Swaledales.

View towards Ullswater from St Sunday Crag *14 September*
Looking north east over the rocky summit of St Sunday Crag
(841m/2,756ft) are fantastic views along Ullswater towards Place Fell
and the hills beyond. On this clear, quiet day it felt as though I was on
top of the world, looking down on everything in miniature. Striding Edge
and Helvellyn would be like Piccadilly Circus on a day like today, but here
there were only a few people, and the peace and spirit of the mountains
could be enjoyed.

ABOVE Boredale *13 October*
I felt a wonderful feeling of wildness as I climbed from Patterdale and wandered up slightly from the route to look down into the glacial valley of Boredale. Red deer stags were roaring across the otherwise silent valley reminding me of Scotland. Unfortunately, I didn't have my binoculars and never did get to see any of the deer as they are so well camouflaged in this terrain. I felt I was now entering a more remote and wild landscape.

RIGHT Evening light over Haweswater *12 October*
Submerged beneath these waters lie the abandoned villages of Measand and Mardale Green, flooded in 1935 when the water level of the natural lake was raised by 29m/95ft by the construction of the Haweswater dam. Understandably, at the time there was public outcry as this was considered to be one of the most picturesque valleys in Westmorland. Despite this human intervention, as I looked across towards the wooded peninsula of The Rigg over the little island of Wood Howe, it felt more remote, tranquil and wild than many other parts of the Lakes that I'd visited.

ABOVE Ice on Hayeswater *7 March*

For those people who have more time and are not rushing the Coast to Coast, just before ascending the Knott, on the way to Kidsty Pike, it is worth taking the path off to the right to catch a glimpse over the col down to Hayeswater. The path eventually leads down to the tiny village of Hartsop near Brother's Water (where there is even a pub for those who want to bail out at this stage). Today, the sun beat down on the icy water below Gray Crag, frozen for months through one of the coldest winters for 30 years, creating interesting melting patterns.

LEFT High Street and Rough Crag from the Straights of Riggindale *7 March*

This is one of my favourite views of this section just before Kidsty Pike summit. Today in the snow, it's hard to imagine Roman soldiers marching along High Street at a height of 8280m/2,716ft, their loftiest route in the country, linking the forts at Ambleside and Brougham. I had earlier seen a snowboarder snaking down the broad slope. Times have changed but thankfully, this high mountain scenery hasn't, and will probably look much the same now as it did in Roman times, unlike the lower slopes and valleys. In the distance is Mardale Ill Bell and Harter Fell.

FAR LEFT Rowantreethwaite Beck, Haweswater
14 October
Although the official route follows the western shore of Haweswater, the eastern shore is worth a visit, despite the quiet road (excluding weekends and bank holidays) which runs close by. If refreshment is needed, the Haweswater Hotel is the only place for miles, and a good excuse for the extended diversion. On the way to the hotel, I stumbled upon this lovely little stone bridge over the combined waters of Rowantreethwaite and Hopegill Becks down by the shore, flanked by two knobbly old ash trees.

LEFT Haweswater Beck *14 October*
I lingered for a while, soaking up the atmosphere, absorbed in my photography, when two Coast to Coasters marched past at an alarmingly fast rate. It seemed such a shame to be hurrying along and missing many of the hidden gems along this route. Admittedly, the destination needs to be reached before nightfall, and this is a long day from Patterdale, but it seems such a pity to miss these things simply because of a tight schedule.

BELOW Thornthwaite Force *14 October*
This was one of those hidden gems. Obscured from view slightly by the trees, it was easy to miss, and I watched as the determined Coast to Coasters marched straight past. It was tricky to find the right composition and I vowed I would return in spring when the surrounding trees would be full of fresh growth and the foliage slightly less dense.

TOP Shap Abbey *12 October*

Shap Abbey was built at the end of the twelfth century at a sheltered and remote site on the bank of the River Lowther. It supported about a dozen monks who combined a life of prayer with work as priests in local communities. The end came in 1540 when the last abbot surrendered the abbey's possessions to the crown. Some of the buildings were converted to a farmhouse, others were demolished or just left. Chickens, then as now, are free to roam its ruins. It is now protected by English Heritage.

BOTTOM Keld near Shap *12 October*

I was surprised by the beauty of this area around Shap. I had always associated Shap with an exposed, bleak section of the M6, usually whizzing past the big Corus limestone works in driving rain and howling gales on my way to Scotland and not giving it a second glance. How wrong I had been! This last bit of Lakeland scenery before we enter the limestone country to the east of Shap is lovely. This is the tiny hamlet of Keld, set against a backdrop of Lakeland fells including the distinctive peak of Kidsty Pike. Nearby is the site of a medieval chapel now owned by the National Trust. I love the Lakes and am always sad to leave , but there is still much outstanding scenery to look forward to, with so much variety. I can't wait to explore it.

Into the Vale of Eden

Shap to Kirkby Stephen
32km / 20 miles

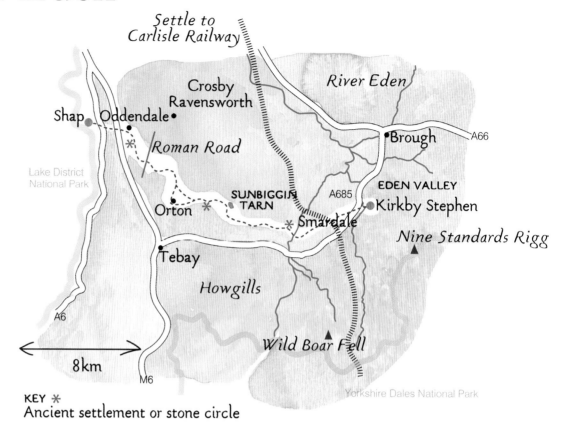

KEY ✳

Ancient settlement or stone circle

This next section is in complete contrast to the Lake District. We are now in limestone country and one of the least-visited parts of Cumbria. For those interested in archaeology, botany or ornithology, they are in for an unexpected treat.

There are a few glacial erratics of red Shap granite boulders scattered over the area , but the permeable bedrock of this limestone plateau means that rivers, tarns and streams are fewer and the scenery is more gently rolling. The plateau is at a height of about 330m/1000ft, covered in verdant pasture in spring and summer for grazing sheep and cows, criss-crossed by drystone walls with a backdrop of the Northern Pennines or Howgills as we approach Orton and the Upper Lune Valley.

Often overlooked as people race past to get to Scotland or the Northern Lakes, this area has a wealth of interest and wild scenery to explore, with spectacular views and a feeling of remoteness, peace and solitude. This corner of what was once named Westmorland is one of the richest areas for prehistoric settlement in the country with finds dating from between 9,000 and 2,000 years ago., There is a profusion of archaeological evidence scattered along the route particularly around Crosby Ravensworth and Smardale, including hut sites, dykes, tumuli, stone circles, cairns and earthworks. There is also evidence of Roman influence, such as the road across Crosby Ravensworth Fell which linked the forts at Low Borrow Bridge and Brougham.

Oddendale Stone Circle *25 April*

Today Oddendale is a quiet hamlet hidden in a cluster of trees well off the beaten track, but thousands of years ago it was a busy place. Within a few miles of this village are the remains of 11 ancient British settlements. Earthworks, tumuli, stone circles and cairns abound, with a Roman road thrown in. Just a few metres off the Coast to Coast track is this stone circle made up of two rings of boulders, not of limestone but of pink Shap granite. Exact knowledge of the origin of this and other stone circles, cairns and tumuli in the area is still sketchy despite the abundant literature on them. The panoramic view shows the backdrop of the northern Pennines behind the trees which hide Oddendale.

There are spectacular examples of limestone pavements on Crosby Ravensworth Fell and the nearby Orton and Great Asby Scars. Many unusual plants and ferns shelter and thrive in the crevices of the limestone, which acts like a giant storage heater, creating miniature rock gardens and adding botanic interest.

For bird lovers, there are conservation areas and designated SSSI's (Sites of Special Scientific Interest) around Crosby Ravensworth Fell, a breeding ground for moorland birds such as golden plover, curlew, redshank and grouse. Sunbiggin Tarn, which sits on a plug of impermeable bedrock, is also an SSSI and an important breeding ground for waterfowl.

The village of Orton can be by-passed but is a pleasant minor diversion and refreshment stop, with a café, pub and even a chocolate factory next to a village green criss-crossed by babbling brooks. After Sunbiggin Tarn, the highlights are the views towards the Howgills and then the descent into Smardale Gill, which is dominated by views to the viaduct along Scandal Beck. This area is also a haven for wildflowers in the summer months as well as of considerable archaeological interest.

Climbing up over Smardale Fell, the views open out across the Eden Valley towards the Yorkshire Dales, Wild Boar Fell and Mallerstang Edge. Glimpses of Nine Standards Rigg can be seen on the skyline near Hartley Fell above Kirkby Stephen, which is still hidden from view. Finally, Kirkby Stephen is reached, the first real town encountered along the route so far. Built along the River Eden, it is a great little market town full of interesting shops and cafes, and worth a stopover for refreshment and replenishment.

LEFT Limestone Pavement, Crosby Ravensworth Fell
17 September
Crossing Crosby Ravensworth Fell is the course of a Roman road, thought to be the first route from London to Scotland. This tranquil area is now a very sensitive conservation area and an important breeding ground for moorland birds, which is why the nearby monument at Black Dub, where King Charles II rested en route from Scotland in 1651, is no longer legally accessible to walkers. Instead of the sound of marching armies, the air now echoes to the calls of curlews, golden plover and lapwings. Over the years, erosion by rain, ice and wind has carved the white limestone into wonderful fissures, knobbles and crevices where unusual plants take refuge. Although slightly off route, even better examples can be seen at nearby Orton or Great Asby Scars, soon to be incorporated into the Yorkshire Dales National Park.

ABOVE The Howgills from Orton Scar *3 June*
Just before the path drops down onto the bridle track from the Appleby Road below Orton Scar, it is worth taking in the wonderful views across the Lune valley near Orton towards the Howgills. They appear like giant pillows piled up against the horizon.

Orton

This pretty village is well worth making a detour. Apart from having a pub and a chocolate factory/café, ideal for refreshments, two streams babble through the village between seventeenth and eighteenth century cottages and a couple of early seventeenth century halls. In 1658, Oliver Cromwell granted a charter for a weekly market, and regular farmers markets are still held here every month. The church with its distinctive sixteenth century white-washed tower is a landmark for miles around.

TOP LEFT Footbridge near the village green *2 June*

BOTTOM LEFT View from Street Lane *25 April*
If you do visit Orton, the chances are you will walk along the B6261 to re-join the track at Knott Lane. If so, you will be rewarded with this lovely view of rolling, verdant pastures backed by the Howgills, at the junction of Street Lane.

ABOVE Knott Lane *2 June*
To rejoin the main route you have to go down this lane flanked with the delicate, dusky pink flowers of water avens in spring. You will also pass the Gamelands stone circle, which is just over the wall on the right. Often overlooked, this is one of the largest stone circles in Cumbria. Made of Shap granite with many stones standing about a metre high, the remaining 33 stones have tumbled from what was thought to be about 40 originally. Artefacts have been found here dating from between 1800-1400 BC.

Sunbiggin Tarn

At Sunbiggin Tarn the limestone landscape suddenly transforms to that of boggy moorland. Clearly the local bedrock is no longer porus limestone. It is an ideal nesting site for waterfowl and for this reason has been designated an SSSI. After a cold, clear night camping at Raisebeck, I awoke to a fantastic, misty dawn. As I approached the tarn, dewdrops were glistening on the cotton grass in the early morning sunlight and every cobweb shone like a jewel. I spent ages on my belly photographing cobwebs, totally absorbed in my photography, the silence only broken by the distinctive sound of snipe fluttering and diving overhead and the shrieks of other birds on the tarn. It is truly a magical place.

LEFT Morning mist rising around Sunbiggin Tarn *3 June 6.18am*
ABOVE Spider's web coated in dew *3 June 6.45am*

FOLLOWING PAGE
Last light at Sunbiggin Tarn in autumn *10 November 5.00pm*

Springtime near Bents Farm *3 June*

At 300m/1,000ft, summer comes late in these isolated places. Despite being June, there is a fresh spring look about this image. The Howgills no longer dominate the skyline, as the Pennines of the Yorkshire Dales start to appear on the horizon. I rounded a corner and was rewarded by the track leading my eye to the sweep of Mallerstang Edge in the distance, giving a feeling of the big, open country of the route ahead. A ewe with her lamb posed on the track to perfect my composition.

Smardale Viaduct and Scandal Beck in spring
near Severals Settlement *3 June*

When I crossed over a stile to follow the substantial limestone wall down to Smardale Gill, I was unaware of the importance of what I was walking past. My eye was drawn by the sweep of the wall leading to an old railway building below, so I did not notice the raised banks and undulations in the ground. I was at the edge of the Severals Village Settlement, thought to be one of the most important prehistoric settlements in Britain. To the archaeologist's eye the raised earthworks, sunken dykes and patterns on the ground are the remains of a complex of former boundaries, farm tracks and traces of ancient

stone huts extending over an area of 100 acres if we include the two other settlements immediately to the north. Severals itself covers three acres. This once bustling area of activity now lies silent and rarely visited apart from the increasing traffic from Coast to Coasters passing through during the spring and summer.

Smardale Viaduct, seen here, once carried the old Tebay-Darlington line but this area is now a peaceful haven for botanists in summer, searching out limestone-loving plants such as bloody cranesbill, dog rose and roseroot. The white flowers of water crowfoot are also abundant in the beck. In spring the hawthorn bushes throughout the valley are bursting with clouds of white May blossom.

TOP LEFT Smardale in autumn *10 November*
I loved this peaceful valley so much that I returned in November to photograph it under a blanket of russet autumn tones. In particular, the hawthorn and rowan trees are now laden with red berries. In the distance there is a dusting of snow on the northern Pennines around Cross Fell.

BOTTOM LEFT Looking across Scandal Beck *10 November*
I strayed off route slightly on a path towards the viaduct in order to photograph the view across the beck and get this wonderful hawthorn tree bursting with bright scarlet berries in the foreground.

TOP RIGHT Climbing up towards Smardale Fell *3 June*
This hawthorn tree looks insignificant as it grows out of the wall flanked with common saxifrage, but for me it was a life saver. It was an extremely hot day in early June, I was desperately thirsty and it created the only tiny bit of shade from the scorching mid-day sun for miles. I took a drink as many other Coast to Coasters passed by complaining of the heat. One man had a large bottle of water swinging from his rucksack and he informed me he was hoping to make Nine Standards Rigg by nightfall. Later, I found his bottle of water along the track. I just hope he made it without being too dehydrated.

BOTTOM RIGHT Views from Limekiln Hill across to Hartley Fell and Mallerstang Edge *15 May*
Dropping down from Smardale Fell to Limekiln Hill, the views east are magnificent as you look across the Eden Valley to Hartley Fell. This spring view takes in the slope of Tailbridge Hill on the end of Mallerstang Edge. Straight ahead beyond Nine Standards is the Yorkshire Dales National Park – the next stage of the walk. But first, you can indulge in refreshments and shopping in the lovely market town of Kirkby Stephen, the first substantial place to spend money since Grasmere.

Kirkby Stephen

This is a modestly-sized old market town of pre-Norman origin which looks much bigger than it actually is. It extends along the A685 which is flanked by chip shops, cafes and shops galore. Its width is limited as the River Eden quietly flows behind it, forming a boundary along its eastern side, while along its western side, hill pastures restrict the spread of buildings.

Once an important refreshment stop for trippers on the way to Blackpool from the North East, now it is a little quieter and frequented by weary Coast to Coasters searching for food and accommodation. However, it remains an important commercial and agricultural centre for a wide area, and is always bustling with activity. At its centre there is a lovely cobbled market square surrounded by interesting buildings, most notably the large parish church of St Stephen, which stands in a peaceful garden behind an impressive arched, cloistered gateway. There are traces of both Saxon and Norman architecture, and in 1240 it was replaced and subsequently enlarged to give the impressive red sandstone structure we see today.

I found Kirkby Stephen to be a friendly place. Mark from Eden Outdoors was a mine of information about the town and its surrounding area. The little café opposite, called The Pink Geranium saved my life after a hot, thirsty afternoon taking photographs. Just as it was closing, proprietors David and Diana Baxter let me in, made me tea, and I spent a good half hour chatting and gleaning more information about their Coast to Coast visitors. Needless to say, they did a roaring trade in blister packs at times when other shops were closed.

Shops lining the A685 below the church of St Stephen *21 April*

Across the Yorkshire Dales

Kirkby Stephen to Richmond
55.5km / 34.5miles

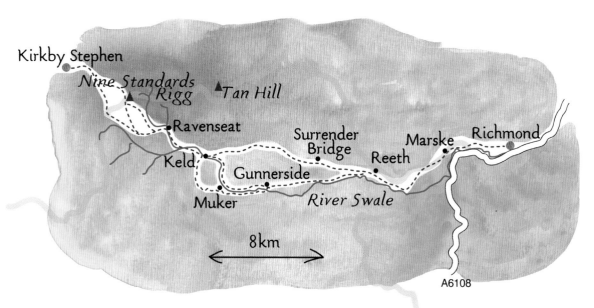

Yorkshire Dales National Park

Leaving Kirkby Stephen, after crossing the River Eden the route passes through the quiet village of Hartley and climbs up past a large limestone quarry along the fell road. The road runs into a bridleway and then the Coast to Coast path splits into three at a strategic signpost.

Now that this walk has become so popular, the Yorkshire Dales National Park has devised colour-coded routes which it advises should be taken depending on the time of year in order to reduce erosion across this sensitive peat moorland. Just beyond the impressive cairns of Nine Standards Rigg, is a trig point at 662m/2,172ft.

This is the watershed of the whole route. From here to the east the streams and rivers flow into the North Sea, our destination, and those to the west into the Irish Sea. We now enter the Yorkshire Dales National Park and

the beauty and wildness of upper Swaledale can be anticipated. The routes converge again at Ney Gill near Whitsundale, soon followed by an oasis of refreshments on a remote farm at Ravenseat. The path leads on to How Edge Scars where Whitsundale Beck has cut an impressive ravine through the limestone and shales. The beck twists and turns near Ovenmouth before following a straighter course to join forces with the River Swale just west of Keld, a tiny, remote village but an important stopover where the Coast to Coast crosses the Pennine Way. This is also the route's half-way point.

The area around Keld is blessed with waterfalls as the Swale flows over the limestone bedrock and follows this beautiful valley all the way through to Richmond. In winter, the snows linger up here, and icicles hang down by the falls which gush fiercely,

Hartley *21 April*
The attractive linear hamlet of Hartley looks lovely in spring with
the beck flowing through, flanked by daffodils and cherry blossom.
It seems a million miles from rumbling quarry lorries working the
nearby Hartley Quarries.

However, for those interested in industrial archaeology, there is much to see. The skeletons of derelict buildings and smelt mills from the boom time of the seventeenth and eighteenth centuries stand amid spoil heaps, and levels, shafts and hushes remain among the plundered veins. Particularly interesting ruins are at Swinner Gill, Blakethwaite and Old Gang Smelt Mills.

Whichever route is taken, they meet just before the large village of Reeth, the principal community of upper Swaledale. With its substantial village green surrounded by cafes, shops and pubs, it is a thriving centre and an important meeting place in this remote valley, full of scattered stone farmhouses and cottages. From mid August to early September, the surrounding moors are covered in a haze of purple heather, which is managed for breeding and shooting grouse.

Beyond Reeth, the Swale is wider and more mature and the landscape is gently rolling, less wild and more wooded. Just beyond Marrick Priory, the route leaves the Swale and heads upwards through the hamlet of Marrick before reaching the tiny village of Marske, which stands in a side valley off the Swale. It is surrounded by deciduous woodland and fringed with limestone cliffs on top of which are the wild heather moors. With its fine

and spring buds arrive much later in May than further down the valley towards Reeth.

Just beyond Keld at Crackpot Hall a decision must be made as to whether to follow the higher, wilder route away from the river and investigate the scarred wastelands of Swaledale's lead mining heritage, or to follow the gentler pastures by the river and walk through Swaledale's flower-rich meadows, which are particularly spectacular in June and July or early spring when the valley is also full of lambs. The two routes are in stark contrast to each other and the former should be avoided in poor visibility.

hall and twelfth century church, it has a quiet charm and is particularly attractive in autumn when the surrounding trees are a riot of colour.

On leaving Marske, the route climbs slightly and follows an Alpine-like, high grassy ledge beneath the limestone cliffs of Applegarth and Whitcliffe Scars, where we leave the Dales national park. The Swale can be seen on the valley bottom before we enter Whitcliffe Woods, a rich, natural woodland full of spring flowers from April to June. Finally, emerging from the woods, there is a distant view of Richmond, dominated by its magnificent Norman castle with the Cleveland Hills and North York Moors beyond.

Richmond is a splendid town, the largest along the route. It is full of unspoilt corners, ancient buildings with interesting shops and cafes. Once again, we meet the now mature river Swale as it flows majestically over a series of falls and cascades right through the town below the castle. It's a fitting end to our passage through the Yorkshire Dales.

LEFT Ascending Faraday Gill *6 March*
Through the mist, trudging up the soggy, snowy path, the first glimpses of a cairn near the Nine Standards can just be seen. I thought it was the top, but was mistaken, as many others would be. It lifted the spirits though, essential in these conditions. Faraday Gill was named after the local family whose youngest son was scientist Michael Faraday (1791-1867), famous for his pioneering work with electromagnetism.

TOP LEFT Permissive path signpost *6 March*
There is a colour-coded route system for this section of the Coast to Coast depending on the time of year in order to minimise damage to the area by erosion. This is the signpost for the red and blue routes, which lead directly to the Nine Standards via Faraday Gill.

ABOVE Nine Standards Rigg *6 March*
Centuries old, and built to endure the harsh conditions this environment must throw at them, no one really knows the origin of these cairns despite many theories. They could be boundary stones as they are on the old county boundary of Westmorland and the North Riding of Yorkshire, which gradually multiplied to the nine we see today. A respected local historian, Dr Stephen Walker wrote the definitive book on the Nine Standards (see Recommended reading), and is about to excavate part of the area as new theories of their purpose are developed.

Today they were in good shape, but they have been in various states of disrepair over the years and in 2005 were renovated. Wainwright describes a magnificent view from here overlooking the Eden Valley, Lakeland, Cross Fell, Mallerstang Ridge and out towards Swaledale. Today, I could hardly see to the end of the cairns, the low cloud was so dense, but my 6ft 5in model gives some idea of their substantial size. About a kilometre beyond here we enter the Yorkshire Dales National Park, but this route is not advised between December and April, so a descent back down was necessary this time in order to take the green route and reduce erosion across the sensitive moorland habitat in these wet, winter conditions.

ABOVE Whitsundale Beck, Ravenseat *15 May*
Ravenseat is a remote farming community with a few scattered houses, but amazingly it's where I enjoyed some of the best cream teas I've ever tasted. This view across the beck in this tranquil spot hides the pile of scones waiting just behind me. On this day I bumped into scores of people from all over the world doing the Coast to Coast, and all calling in for a cream tea at Ravenseat farmhouse, served very efficiently by Amanda Owen and her children. I vowed I would be back. It's not surprising that business is booming, as these are the first refreshments after many miles of remote, peat moorland from Kirkby Stephen. It was a great example of how this route has pumped funds directly into what must be a difficult livelihood from sheep farming in these remote parts. I later discovered Amanda now has a luxurious shepherd's hut which she rents out for accommodation.

RIGHT View from How Edge Scars *15 May*
Suddenly the path skirts the top of How Edge Scars, and there is a wonderful view down into a deep ravine called Boggle Hole (boggle is a North Country word for a ghost). High on the ledge is a great place for a coffee stop; this view took me by surprise and must be relished not rushed.

Ovenmouth *28 October*
Further downstream, on a sharp bend in Whitsundale Beck, is Ovenmouth. There is a great viewpoint looking west towards a scattering of field barns and remote farmhouses up the gully of Reynoldson Sike. In the strong autumn sunlight, I was suddenly caught in a squally shower when taking this picture, hence the blobs of rain on my lens blurring the top of the image slightly.

View east from Cotterby Scar *28 October*
Flanked at this time of year by hawthorn laden with crimson berries, this shows the higher route along Cotterby Scar. From here there are lovely views of the landscape surrounding Keld, still hidden in the dip beyond the verdant fields. The snaking road over the hill leads straight there and must be a welcome sight for many a Coast to Coast walker.

Wain Wath Force

The top of Swaledale is characterised by a series of waterfalls as the Swale tumbles down from the high peaty moorland through the limestone bedrock. Below Cotterby Scar is Wain Wath Force, more easily accessible than some and well worth a visit. I'd previously been there in June, when the water was a feeble dribble after a very dry spring. I thought I'd return when the River Swale was in full spate. After a wet autumn the brown peat-stained water was gushing over the ledge, creating a natural foam which can be seen trapped between the boulders.

LEFT Spring, Wain Wath Force *17 June*

BOTTOM LEFT Autumn, Wain Wath Force *28 October*

BELOW East Gill Force, Keld *1 February*
Keld should be a place of celebration, as this is not only
a place for rest and refreshment but the half-way point of
the Coast to Coast route. It is also where the route crosses
the Pennine Way near to East Gill Force. I visited this waterfall
after our coldest winter in many years. Ice formations
adorned the surrounding rocks, making it extremely difficult
to approach, but I persevered and managed a few close-ups
of these spectacular natural sculptures.

LEFT Kisdon Gorge *12 May*
Ascending the cart track to the right of East Gill Force, we leave those heading along the Pennine Way to go left as we carry on east towards the North Sea. This is the high route through Swaledale and lead mining country, but before we reach the bleak landscape of old mines and spoil heaps, there are some wonderful views along the way. This is a great view down into Kisdon Gorge in spring when the river is not yet hidden from view by the foliage but flanked by fresh green growth. This gorge was formed when the melting glacial rivers cut out a new course for the Swale when its former course to the west was blocked by glacial debris.

ABOVE Retrospective view of Keld in spring *12 May*
Blackthorn blossom lines the track which leads to the Tan Hill road, and Keld basks under tranquil blue skies and puffy white clouds as I ascend towards Crackpot Hall.

Crackpot Hall

The sad ruins of Crackpot Hall stand in a spectacular location high on the hillside. The seventeenth century farmhouse was built by Lord Wharton for his gamekeeper, who managed red deer which then roamed the wooded hillsides. Sadly, in the 1950's, subsidence from the nearby mining activities meant the farmhouse had to be abandoned.

It is at this point along the route that a decision must be made as to whether to follow the high level, more exposed route to Reeth through the ruins and spoil heaps of the lead mining industry, or to follow the gentler pastures of the Swale. For this book I'll do both to ensure the highlights of both are covered. There is also a third option to follow the road from Keld to Muker via Thwaite, where equally, the scenery does not disappoint. Their different landscapes offer great contrasts.

View down the valley from Crackpot Hall *12 May*
As we approach the ruins of Crackpot Hall, there is a wonderful view straight down the valley towards Muker following the course of the River Swale below Kisdon Side as it flows southwards, showing the alternative river route. In May the landscape is fresh and green with new growth and the blue sky is reflected in the Swale as it meanders its way towards the tiny village of Muker, which we can see in the distance.

Field Barns

Taking the gentler route through the meadows and pastures alongside the Swale, we pass many attractive field barns, a feature of this area. These limestone barns were built in the meadows away from the farmhouses to store hay produced in summer to feed cattle and sheep through the bleak winter months. Unlike other areas, where livestock was brought to the main farm through winter, here small numbers of livestock were kept on the ground floor of the shippon and the hay above. This was an efficient system where the hay never left the field where it grew, and manure from the livestock was then spread back onto the same fields to fertilise them.

ABOVE Barn near Keld on a frosty morning in May *12 May*
An unusually cold night in May produced a heavy ground frost, particularly visible on the shady hillside beyond. It was the red painted doors and windows which attracted me to this characteristic two-storey barn in such a glorious spot.

TOP RIGHT The same barn near Keld in June *17 June*
Just one month later, and the landscape has quickly transformed into a riot of greens. The lush meadow is filled with buttercups and the hillside has exploded with fresh growth and is covered in May blossom.

BOTTOM LEFT Barn near Muker in hay meadows by the Swale *17 June*
The hay meadows near Muker in June are magnificent and the Coast to Coast route runs right through if you are walking the lower route down from Crackpot Hall. This sea of yellow is probably at its best mid June and it is left until the flowers have set their seeds; the farmers are then allowed to cut the meadow in July.

BOTTOM RIGHT Path to Muker through the hay meadows *16 June*
Walking south to Muker from Crackpot Hall, you can glimpse this lovely village across the green and yellow. The promise of a good pub, tea shop, galleries and food make it even more like paradise.

BELOW Squeezer Stiles *17 June*

Walking the lower route through Swaledale there are endless squeezer stiles through the many walls to negotiate. Some of the gates have incredibly strong springs and can be quite vicious.

RIGHT Early morning dew on buttercups, clover and meadow cranesbill *17 June*

Swaledale is famed for its hay meadows. The Haytime Project hopes to restore more than 500 acres across the national park by collecting seeds from existing meadows and spreading them in nearby fields. These meadows are extremely rich in wildflowers. Apart from the abundant buttercups, there are meadow cranesbill, lady's mantle, crosswort, pignut and bluebells, to name just a few. Botanical surveys have shown up to 30 different species in a single square metre. Below are a few images which I managed to capture early one morning.

Muker

In the ninth century, Swaledale produced half the lead mined in Yorkshire and by the sixteenth and seventeenth centuries this region was booming as lead from these mines was used to cover cathedrals, churches and castle roofs all over the country. In those days Muker and many other villages had both larger populations and greater wealth than many other equivalent rural communities.

In 1829 lead prices dropped because of cheaper foreign imports, and the mines began to close. Families were forced out to work in the Durham coalfields or northern mills, and the population in the valley dropped dramatically, leaving sheep farming as the main surviving industry, only recently supplanted by tourism. Wool and sheep farming has been an important industry in Swaledale since monastic times and knitting, often undertaken by miners and their families, was the second industry of the dale. The black-faced, white-nosed Swaledale sheep which we see everywhere across the Yorkshire Dales (including on the rooftop of a Muker craft gallery!) were ideal as they could withstand the harsh winter conditions.

BELOW Muker from the south west *16 June*
Although the route does not go directly through Muker, it is a pleasant place to take a rest day and enjoy the nearby meadows, hills and amenities. This view shows the village below the mass of Black Hill. The lower route of the Coast to Coast skirts its base, and the higher route through the mine workings runs through the bleak moors behind it above Swinner Gill.

In contrast to the drystone walls, meadows and field barns along the Swale, the following few images are taken on the high route through lead mining country. It's hard to imagine that quiet Swaledale once produced much of the nation's lead. Mined since Roman times, mining techniques changed over the years, but the destructive technique of 'hushing' peaked in the mid-eighteenth century and is responsible for much of the scarred landscape we see today. This technique involved damming becks and then releasing torrents of water to remove soil and stones, in order to reveal the precious lead veins.

The hillsides between Crackpot and Surrender Bridge would have been noisy industrial hives of activity.

Today the noise is that of moorland birds rather than of machinery, but the remains of flues, rail tracks, tunnels, smelt mills and crushing machinery lie abandoned along the route,provoking the imagination of the passer-by. On close inspection, I found traces of lead ore in the spoil heaps, so the miners left us some of their precious commodity. More importantly, they also left us the excellent network of bridleways, tracks and footpaths which walkers, cyclists and horse-riders can now enjoy.

ABOVE Field patterns near Gunnerside *12 May*
This is a great example of field patterns and barns near Gunnerside, where the Coast to Coast river route runs. Slightly backlit by the sun, the verdant fields and dark walls make a lovely abstract composition.

FAR LEFT Swinner Gill *22 April*
At the top of Swinner Gill lie the ruins of East Grain smelt mill. Just below it a waterfall tumbles over a mossy ledge and next to that a mine level can be seen disappearing into the hillside.

A closer view of the waterfall shows the incredibly vivid green moss which flourishes as the water from East Grain tumbles over. (Just up off the track is a well-hidden cave known locally as Swinner Gill Kirk. This was used by Catholics and non-conformists at a time when such religious gatherings were illegal, resulting in death if discovered)

TOP Old Gang Smelt Mill *23 April*
This image shows the old smelt mill in its setting with Old Gang Beck winding through the spoil tips of Mill Gill. It operated until 1880, and the Old Gang Mines in Hard Level Gill were one of the most productive in the area. Now, the ruins of this smelt mill are stabilised and preserved, and certainly worth wandering around.

BOTTOM Surrender Mill *28 August*
Stormy light on an August afternoon falls on this ruined smelting mill near Surrender Bridge. This is a fascinating area for anyone interested in industrial archaeology. From studying these relics, organisations such as the Northern Mine Research Society and Earby Mine Research Group have built up knowledge of early mining techniques, tracking the changes in the way lead ore was extracted. The old peat store columns can still be seen among the ruins on the right of the main building.

View south across the Swale from Reeth *28 August*
The route along the Swale and the higher route, which eventually leads down Skelgate Lane, converge on the western fringes of Reeth. Early morning light gave this lovely view south across the meandering Swale over towards Harkerside Moor.

Reeth

Reeth stands at the junction of Swaledale and Arkengarthdale, and was once an important centre for the mining industry, hence its larger size and title as the capital of mid Swaledale. Apart from mining and knitting, it also contained the principal market for the local farming community, and it still boasts a grand village green surrounded by pubs, shops, cafes, and hotels. Good reason that it's such a great place to overnight before the next leg of the journey on to Richmond.

The Black Bull and Ice Cream Parlour *28 August*
Two of the many places for refreshement just off the village green.

View of Reeth and Arkengarthdale *28 August*
The view of Reeth from the moors just above Grinton shows how this settlement stands at the mouth of the more remote Arkengarthdale and below the disused chert quarries of Fremington Edge. Chert, a hard, blue flint-like rock used for paving stones, was quarried here until 1950. You can also clearly see Reeth's lovely, large village green.

Calver Hill *28 August*
Looking across to Calver Hill (470m/1,542ft) from the grouse moors above Grinton, we can see the terrain through which the higher Coast to Coast route passes. Just below the heather moorland are lush green fields flanked by many limestone walls, picked out in the early morning light.

ABOVE Marrick Priory *11 May*

Beyond Reeth and Grinton, the twelfth century Marrick Priory stands beside the River Swale. It was occupied by Benedictine nuns in 1154 until it was dissolved by Henry VIII in 1540. Ironically, one stormy night in 1535 one of Henry's court favourites, Isabella Beaufort, fled London and sheltered here, disguised as a pageboy. The romantic ruin even attracted the attention of JWM Turner, who made a sketch of its ancient buildings. With only the tower remaining, it later became the parish church and Abbey Farm, but in the 1960s it was converted by the Ripon Diocese into an outdoor education centre with additional buildings.

Sunset near Marske *12 September*

I captured this most spectacular sunset near Marske, looking towards Swaledale. The whole sky appeared to be on fire. There are few sunsets like this in a year, and often they appear when you are in an inappropriate place or without a camera. This time I was lucky.

The River Swale from East Applegarth *4 April*

Beyond Marske, the route crosses a lovely high grassy ledge below
limestone scars through a few farms above the Swale. This is just
one of the views from the ledge below Whitcliffe Scar before entering
the woods. On this stormy day in April, the River Swale takes on the
colour of the slate grey sky as it winds its way through the green fields
on the way to Richmond. Sadly, we have now left the Yorkshire Dales
National Park, but the delights of Richmond are just round the corner.

Richmond *4 April*

After a pleasant walk through Whitcliffe Woods, the path emerges before the distant town of Richmond with its magnificent Norman keep dominating the old streets and buildings below. It is the only big town along the walk. Apart from exploring its fascinating history and buildings, it has the necessary pubs, cafes, outdoor gear shops, and many others waiting to supply you with all those essentials you need to replenish and refresh. On this incredibly clear spring day, the distant Cleveland Hills stand out despite being 25 miles away across the next section of the walk, the Vale of Mowbray.

The Vale of Mowbray

Richmond to Ingleby Cross
37km / 23miles

Osmotherley
Extension, an extra 5km / 3miles

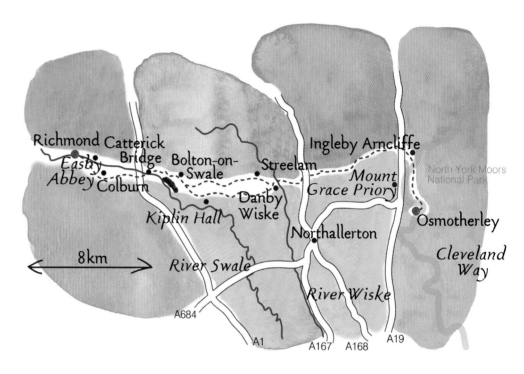

I was led to believe that the next section after leaving Richmond, the Vale of Mowbray, would be dull, flat and tedious. However, I was pleasantly surprised. It is fairly flat, but I found there was much to photograph.

The underlying geology is Triassic sandstones and mudstones, with the overlying soil formed from glacial deposits. Consequently, it is extremely rich and fertile agricultural land, used for arable crops such as rape and barley as well as large expanses of meadows for cows and sheep.

Leaving the limestone country behind near Richmond, in the east of the region houses tend to be built of Yorkshire sandstone with terracotta-coloured pantile roofs. Depending on the time of year the scenery is very rewarding, with tranquil, flower-decked lanes flanked by low, well-maintained hedgerows, big sky views and, being quieter and off the beaten track, lots of nature to observe if you can tune into it. However, if conditions are wet then it's likely to be a mud bath along many sections.

The first treat is Easby Abbey just a mile out of Richmond. Although not officially on the route, the substantial ruins are well maintained by English Heritage and worth a visit. The tiny village of Colburn is soon reached after

Richmond from Holly Hill *27 October*
From Holly Hill on the south side of Richmond, there are great views of the castle dominating the town. Holly Hill can be reached by climbing up from the route which runs alongside the Swale's southern banks. Inquisitive sheep made a useful foreground for my photographs, as the sun set on this lovely October afternoon.

passing through woodland alongside the Swale which is full of spring flowers in April and May, and by Colburn Beck, along which red campion, wild garlic, forget-me-nots and bluebells grow in profusion.

We say goodbye to the Swale as we approach Bolton-on-Swale, where the now broad, meandering river takes a swing southwards away from the route. Soon after, at Ellerton Hill, there is another choice of route, either to follow minor roads through small plantations to the villages of Streetlam and Danby Wiske, or to take a detour to visit Kiplin Hall and then cross footpaths through the low lying fields.

It is here that the lowest point of the Coast to Coast is reached, at around 33.5m/110ft in the heart of the Vale of Mowbray. In May, this area is marked by yellow rape fields. This soft landscape, with scattered farms on slightly raised ground of tiny green islands above a sea of yellow against a deep blue sky, is nevertheless uplifting.

During dry periods in late summer, the landscape changes across the Vale of Mowbray and is dominated by machinery frantically harvesting the hay and scattering the stubble fields with large round bales. Depending on how they've been worked, the fields now become a patchwork of colour, greens, golds and brown.

On reaching Ingleby Arncliffe, the Cleveland Hills dominate the views ahead and the flat, easy walking is over. At Ingleby Cross, we enter the North York Moors National Park. If there is no accommodation in Ingleby, then nearby Osmotherly is a fitting end to this section, but requires a short, sharp, climb up through Arncliffe and South Woods past Arncliffe Hall. It is a good warm up and a great place to stay overnight before the exertions needed to cross the North York Moors to reach journey's end in the days ahead.

FAR LEFT View of Richmond from the east
5 November
This morning view shows how the 30m/100ft castle keep dwarfs the Chapel of Holy Trinity and obelisk in the market square on the right of the picture. It towers above a labyrinth of alleys and streets between old buildings in this beautiful town. The market place, cobbled in 1771, is the largest horseshoe-shaped market in England. Many houses were built around the Georgian period, as this was an era of great prosperity for the town.

ABOVE The River Swale in Richmond
5 November
Not only is Richmond blessed with the nooks and crannies of old streets and buildings to explore, but also, thundering right through the middle, is the now mature River Swale, complete with a beautiful set of natural rocky limestone ledges and cascades. Many people use this |area below the castle for recreation, and a delightful little hut called Barries Café by the falls conveniently sells hot drinks and snacks.

LEFT Station Bridge in autumn *5 November*
Framed by golden beech leaves, this impressive bridge spans the Swale on the eastern side of town near the old Tudor-style railway station, which was once the terminus of a branch line from Darlington. The station has recently been tastefully converted into a heritage and community centre.

TOP LEFT Spring flowers near Colburn Beck *14 May*

On the approach to Colburn, the path runs alongside Colburn Beck. In May it is flanked by lovely spring flowers such as red campion, forget-me-nots and bluebells.

BOTTOM LEFT Colburn Beck in autumn *27 October*

The old village of Colburn is tiny in contrast to the large modern estate nearby, consisting of a few cottages, a ford, a pub and Colburn Hall. The hall is difficult to see from the path, but is a rebuilt Tudor mansion with a separate manor house. Green lichen coats a hawthorn bush as it hangs over Colburn Beck near to White Cottage in the centre of the village, and the yellows and golds of the autumn leaves are reflected back into the water. Today there were no walkers, but in summer the little village is transformed with hundreds of Coast to Coasters plodding through. I'm constantly reminded how important it is to respect these quiet places and their inhabitants and not cause too much disruption, especially now this walk is so popular.

BELOW St Mary's Church, Bolton-on-Swale *5 November*

Late afternoon sun brings out the colour of the sandstone blocks in the Gothic tower of this church built in the early fourteenth century. Most people, however, head for the churchyard to look at the memorial dedicated to Henry Jenkins, who reputedly lived to be a remarkable 169. Supposedly born at nearby Ellerton in 1500, he claimed on oath that he remembers carrying arrows to the archers at the battle of Flodden Field in 1513 at the age of 12. He certainly died in 1670 after a mixed career that included serving as butler to Lord Coniers of Hornby Castle, salmon fishing, thatching and, later in life, begging for alms. Two other famous/notorious characters born here were the Gunpowder Plotters John and Kit Wright.

ABOVE Kiplin Hall *27 October*
Those who take to the fields will be rewarded by a chance to have a peek at Kiplin Hall and possible refreshments in the tea shop, open between February and October along with the gardens and grounds. Kiplin Hall is one of the finest examples of red brick Jacobean architecture in Britain. It was built as a hunting lodge in 1620 for George Calvert, James I's Secretary of State, who was born at Kiplin where his father leased land and bought the estate in 1619.

RIGHT Tree House in Streetlam *12 May*
It's often the little things that you remember along a walk. I was amused by (and envious of) this wonderful tree house on the corner as you enter Streetlam. All it needed was a B&B sign and I'm sure some Coast to Coasters (including myself) would be tempted.

TOP Lazenby Hall near Danby Wiske *12 May*
Danby Wiske is actually the lowest point of the
Coast to Coast walk being only 33.5m/110ft above
sea level. Across the River Wiske lies Lazenby
Hall, seen here amid a sea of yellow rape fields
at this time of year. Built in the 1620's, the hall is
now a farmhouse, but it is reputed that there is a
secret tunnel running from the hall under the river
to the church. As with all secret tunnels, the exact
whereabouts is a mystery.

**BOTTOM Rape fields near Lazenby Hall and
Danby Wiske** *12 May*
This is a great time of year to be crossing the Vale
of Mowbray, surrounded by these glorious yellow
fields. Unless, that is, you are allergic to rape pollen.

LEFT Approaching Sydal Lodge *27 October*
As we walk towards Sydal Lodge, the Cleveland Hills get nearer and the North York Moors beckon. Our level walking will soon be over.

ABOVE Ingleby Arncliffe and Ingleby Cross *15 June*
This is a pretty, peaceful, two-part village, despite being stuck between two major busy roads. Now at the end of the Vale of Mowbray, weary walkers gather around the cross waiting for transport by one of the bag-carrying companies to their accommodation for the night. Behind them is the Bluebell Inn, a popular place to stay. The cross, which is also the village war memorial, is a replacement of the old one which blew down in the gales of 2005.

Walking through South Wood in winter

28 November

If there is no accommodation at Ingleby, then nearby Osmotherley is a great place to head for and only slightly off route. These are not the conditions in which normal Coast to Coasters would be walking. I was heading for the North York Moors to capture recent heavy snowfall, only to be beaten back by more heavy snow the following day. These atmospheric misty conditions were along the route through South Wood on the way to Beacon Hill.

A winter's evening in Osmotherley *28 November*
At last Osmotherley is reached and the warm glow of lights on a cold, snowy evening offer comfort. Food and accommodation were welcome in these freezing conditions. A passing car lights up the old village cross, creating traffic trails in my photograph as I dive into the nearest pub to defrost.

This is an ideal stopover before the start of the challenging but spectacular North York Moors section. It is a lovely little village complete with a market cross, village store and information point, pubs, chip shop, café and even a walking shop. Constructed of traditional Yorkshire sandstone and pantiled roofs, many of the houses were built in the early 1800's to provide accommodation for workers in the nearby alum quarries and jet mines, although it was originally a market village.

The North York Moors

Osmotherley to Robin Hood's Bay
80km/50miles

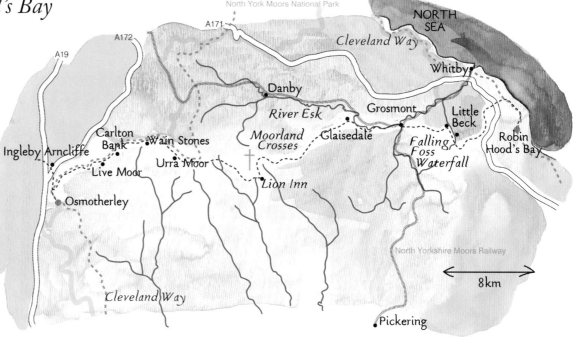

The final section of the route through the North York Moors National Park passes over different geological formations, which in turn throw up a fascinating variety of land use and scenery. Rising steeply up from the Cleveland Plain and the Vale of Mowbray, the North York Moors are an expanse of high heather moorland, dissected by lush green valleys scattered with sandstone houses with red pantile roofs.

In mid-August to early September, the heather forms a vast purple carpet and smells intensely of honey. It is a peaceful haven as there are relatively few roads with little traffic or industry. It is littered with ancient moorland crosses, tracks and prehistoric relics, with evidence of human occupation dating back over 10,000 years. The moorland slopes were more wooded and important hunting grounds, but during the Neolithic and Bronze Ages of around 5,000-2,000 BC, much of the original woodland was cleared. The climate was warmer and drier then, enabling people to inhabit the higher moorland throughout the year.

The geology is dominated by rocks from the Jurassic period. With fluctuations in sea level, bands of different rocks, varying from shales to sandstones and limestones, were laid down before being uplifted and tilted southwards during the intervening millenia.

Rivers ran down the sides of the moorland dome and carved out deep dales in the soft shales beneath giving the lush verdant valleys. Across the north of the region, younger rocks such as limestone were eroded away, revealing the older layers of ironstones, shales or sandstones below.

With poor drainage, sandstones form acid soils which are deficient in nutrients, creating peat bogs formed from the decaying sphagnum moss, which thrives in these conditions. As peat levels are raised and dry out, heather and bilberry invade and flourish. The North York Moors National Park covering 554 square miles (1,436 sq km) contains one of the largest expanses of heather moorland in the UK. At Robin Hood's Bay, the sea has cut into the dome of Jurassic rocks revealing patterns of curving "onion skin" layers of shale, with the outer ring of tough sandstone forming the 'cheeks' at either side of the bay.

On leaving Osmotherley with its pretty sandstone cottages and red-tiled roofs, the Coast to Coast joins up with the 108-mile Cleveland Way National Trail. As the route climbs up to Live Moor, it is dominated by heather moorland with views west across the Cleveland Plain over the wooded slopes below. As we look down across the plain, the patchwork of

Path to Carlton Moor from Live Moor *20 August*
High winds at altitude have formed these lovely wispy cloud
formations which we can see over Carlton Moor. Just before the
summit of Live Moor at 312m/1,024ft, and marked by a broad cairn
of scattered stones built on a tumulus, the terrain levels out for a
while. This ridge is also a watershed between the Ouse and the Tees.
On the far left, we can just see the pimple of Roseberry Topping,
a distinctively-shaped hill much changed by quarrying. This mini
Matterhorn will be seen frequently over the next few miles until Danby
High Moor is reached beyond the Lion Inn.

fields are like a giant multi-coloured blanket spread
across the landscape northwards to the horizon and
not-so-distant industrial Teeside. These views stay with
you until you head up Urra Moor from Clay Bank, finally
leaving the escarpment as we head over Round Hill
towards Farndale Moor.

Along the route, particularly near Clay Bank, Carlton
Moor and Cringle Moor and around the head of
Farndale and Rosedale, there are glimpses of industrial
archaeology left by the remains of the mining of
ironstone or alum.

Alum, which comes from a frost-resistant clay, was
an important chemical for use in tanning, dyeing and
papermaking. Until 1600, the Catholic Church had a
monopoly on the process and it was exported at great
expense from Rome, but then a Yorkshire landowner,
Sir Thomas Chaloner, found this same clay on the
moors. Smuggling over craftsmen from Rome, he
discovered a process that involved boiling up the ore
for hours with urine and seaweed. Production lasted for
252 years until cheaper alternative sources meant local
output ceased in 1867.

Ironstone had been smelted for iron ore for around
2,000 years, but there was a boom during the medieval
period driven by monks who had some 120 small
scale furnaces scattered around the moors. During the
Industrial Revolution, production was on a much larger
scale and in 1861, the ironstone railway which contours
round the head of Farndale above Rosedale was built.
This bleak line, often blocked by snow, was used until
January, 1929.

Jet, a fossilised wood from monkey puzzle trees
some 180 million years old, was found in narrow seams
inland from Whitby and along the coast near Robin
Hood's Bay. This had been a valuable commodity since
pre-Roman times, as it was easily carved to make shiny
black jewellery. It became particularly fashionable in
Victorian times when Queen Victoria favoured it while in
mourning after the death of Prince Albert.

At Bloworth Crossing beyond Urra Moor, the bed of

the old ironstone railway takes our path on a nice easy gradient around the head of Farndale Moor to the Lion Inn at Blakey, the first campsite for many miles with the possibility for evening refreshment. All along, there are great views into Farndale.

The head of Rosedale is crossed and the route passes several moorland crosses around the exposed Danby High Moor at a height of around 423m/1,388ft. The route branches off west past the shooting lodge of Trough House with glorious views down into Great Fryup Dale, keeping high on Glaiseale Moor until it suddenly drops down into Glaisedale village, where it crosses the River Esk at Beggar's Bridge.

Now off the exposed moors, the walk continues at a low level through lovely sheltered woodland along the River Esk, past Egton Manor until it reaches the railway enthusiasts' dream village of Grosmont. Here visitors can take a trip back in time, where steam trains puff on the North Yorkshire Moors Railway and whistles toot as passengers scramble onto trains bound for Whitby or Pickering.

A steep climb out of Grosmont up Fair Head Lane finally gives glimpses of the North Sea as it approaches the open moorland, past the ancient Low and High Bride Stones on Sleights Moor. With the North Sea now temptingly close, the path drops down off the moors once again at Littlebeck and delves through woodland past Falling Foss waterfall.

On the last leg of the journey, there is a final climb out of woods before reaching Hawsker. From nearby Hawsker Bottom the path reaches the North Sea at Maw Wyke Hole. Before you can celebrate and dip your toes, there is a delightful level cliff top coastal path running south east along the Cleveland Way, with magnificent sea views along the top of shale cliffs and down below onto the shore platforms, so characteristic of this stretch of the coast.

Tantalisingly, our final destination of Robin Hood's Bay is not spotted until we round a headland for the final kilometre. Robin Hood's Bay, with its quaint cottages, steep cobbled alleyways and rocky beach, clings attractively to this unstable coastline. It is a fitting and charming end to a fantastic walk.

Views from Carlton Moor summit *20 August*

Taken in mid-August when the heather was in perfect condition, the summit views looking out over the patchwork of fields of the Cleveland Plain are spectacular. On the distant right industrial Teeside can be seen. The view must be similar to that seen by the gliders from the Newcastle and Teeside Gliding Club which soar along this ridge.

Paramotoring from Carlton Bank *11 September*

On the day I turned up there was a gathering of paramotoring enthusiasts. As well as gliding, Carlton Bank is a popular hang-gliding and paragliding site with easy access by road. Having been a hang-glider pilot in the past, I could appreciate the attraction for taking off on ridge lift, catching a few thermals and soaring like a bird over the Cleveland Plain and North York Moors. A nice flat top for landing, complete with café and car park makes it all perfect. Just before this pilot took off he let me feel the weight of the paramotor. For me, it was impossibly heavy to lift, and a surprise that he got airborne at all! It's much easier without a motor.

View of Hasty Bank from Cold Moor *23 August*

The descent from Cold Moor at 402m/1,319ft gives great views over to the Wain Stones, a sandstone outcrop of boulders, crags and pinnacles on Hasty Bank, with Urra Moor beyond. On close inspection of the OS map, there are hundreds of disused tips marked both below the Wain Stones and along the base of Urra Moor.

The Wain Stones *12 August*

There are few rock climbing areas in the North York Moors, so this little outcrop is very popular. In fact, on one of the days I was here I met Alan Hinks, the well-known Yorkshire mountaineer, who was giving lessons to a group of teenagers. This is a great spot for your lunch, sheltering from the rain, taking photographs or even having a scramble. However lovely walking along the heather clad escarpments are, this little crag makes a pleasant change. As I look west back to Cold Moor, a chink of sunlight breaks through the stormy sky and illuminates the base of the rocks.

Hasty Bank *12 August*

Turning east to walk along Hasty Bank, the same chink of sunlight created this dramatic scene as it lit up the moorland, while everywhere else was cast in shadow and the sky was a dark, inky blue. I love this kind of light and I had only seconds to get the right composition before the light had gone… and the rain arrived.

FAR LEFT Moorland Crosses, Young Ralph Cross *21 August*
The North York Moors are littered with moorland crosses, and particularly the area around Rosedale Head and Danby High Moor. Many date back from the seventh century, when Christianity began to spread in this area. They were used in medieval times to guide travellers across the moors. Some have lost their tops but pictured here is Young Ralph Cross, which was adopted as the symbol for the North York Moors National Park which was designated in 1952.

LEFT Fat Betty *21 August*
Not far from Young Ralph Cross is the little stumpy white stone, named Fat Betty, a less elegant cross which brings to my mind the Yorkshire Fat Rascal, a delicious currant bun found in Betty's Tearooms in Harrogate and York. On the subject of food, it is customary to leave a few sweets on Fat Betty for fellow travellers, ensuring a fresh supply of goodies is always found on the stone. It stems from an ancient tradition of food, coins or drink to be left, in thanks for safe travel. What a great idea. It obviously still works as I found some boiled sweets waiting for me. To continue tradition, I left some mints in return.

BOTTOM Rainbow over Trough House *21 August*
There is much evidence of Bronze Age settlement in this area. Modern man is obviously softer than his ancestors, and the only settlement around here now is a shooting cabin called Trough House. There were squally showers blowing across the moor as I walked towards the cabin on the way to Glaisedale. The light across the moor was fantastic, but the wind incredibly strong, making photography difficult. As I was armed with only a tripod the grouse were safe, and I was tempted to shelter inside the cabin but it was locked.

Great Fryup Dale *21 August*

Crossing through an area of nineteenth century coal mining tips now covered in bracken, heather and bilberry, this lovely view opens out as we look down Great Fryup Dale. I love the name of this dale although it's named after the beautiful Norse Goddess Freya and 'up' means a small valley, and has nothing to do with the traditional Yorkshire breakfast. The lumpy area on the left, which looks like a collection of drumlins, is actually grassed over spoil heaps from the mines and is known as The Hills. These give fascinating shadows when the light falls obliquely across them.

Glaisedale Rigg *12 August*

This fine track across Glaisedale Rigg is great in August when the heather is out. A gently descending track to Glaisedale village, it gives great views of the Glaisedale valley and highlights the difference in the landscape between the wilder moorland, with its sparse vegetation, and the lush green valley below, scattered with farms and fields of grazing animals.

Farndale from Blakey Moor *22 August*

The railway was built in 1861 to carry the high-grade magnetic iron ore from the mines in Rosedale over the moors to join up with main lines in Cleveland and then on to the blast furnaces in Teeside and Durham. This must have been a wild and desolate place to work for the staff on Blakey Moor who controlled the operation. Now, it provides a speedy route for walkers. Just past the embankment near Dale Head on Blakey Moor are glimpses of the lovely green valley of Farndale, once threatened with conversion into a reservoir to provide water for Hull.

Grosmont Station

At the confluence of two rivers, the Esk and Murk Esk, Grosmont is situated in a wooded dell and all the roads down into it are very steep. Fortunately, it has another transport link, the wonderful North Yorkshire Moors Railway. In 1965, it was saved from closure by the North Yorkshire Moors Railway Preservation Society and today it is a great success, providing a major tourist attraction with its steam trains running 18 miles between Whitby and Pickering on one of the loveliest rail lines in the country.

LEFT *11 August*
There is hustle and bustle as a train arrives. A good spot as the pretty station café serves great snacks, and the local shops and post office are nearby at the end of the platform.

RIGHT *11 August*
Peace returns to the platform. The wonderful 1950s-style blue and white painted buildings are in pristine condition, indicating that the business continues to thrive.

TOP Fair Head Lane *11 August*
Looking back down the lane, the steep climb out of Grosmont is rewarded by fabulous retrospective views over a patchwork of fields towards the distant moorlands you have recently trudged over.

ABOVE Wood anemone in Scarry Wood, Little Beck *21 April*
This is a brilliant woodland walk alongside the Little Beck stream. In April, when I was here, there was wood sorrel, wood anemone and primroses nestling among the roots of enormous beech trees, not yet in leaf. I could see evidence of wild garlic and bluebells, which would be a wonderful sight in May. On this sunny afternoon the natural woodland of beech, oak, ash and hazel was full of birdsong, and the trickling burble from the nearby beck made it all very tranquil.

RIGHT The Hermitage *21 April*
The path climbs away from the stream and then suddenly you are faced by this massive boulder with a wonderful carved entrance and the letters GC 1790 just above it. This is The Hermitage, which was carved out by George Chubb, a Littlebeck schoolmaster. Nobody quite knows why, but maybe he wanted a place where he could escape to avoid the pressures of eighteenth century living. Nowadays, we have allotments and sheds.

LEFT CENTRE Falling Foss Waterfall *21 April*

As I rounded a corner in what seemed like the middle of nowhere, I thought I was hallucinating. Obsessed with tea shops and feeling very thirsty, I thought I could see tables, chairs and parasols in what looked like a garden café. And there, totally unexpected, was the most delightful little tea garden at a place called Midge Hall. Wainwright described it as a museum, but it was originally built as a gamekeeper's cottage in the 1780's, and was known as Mrs Robinson's Tea Garden in the early 1900's. It has recently re-opened after nearly 50 years and, situated right next to Falling Foss waterfall, it is spectacularly located. Naturally, I had to test it out. Unfortunately, the waterfall was only a mere trickle after a fairly dry spring. I'd love to return in autumn when the water levels are higher and the woodland canopy is golden. I just hope the tea shop is still open.

ABOVE Sea cliffs near Far Jetticks *22 April*

Looking back north along the route is this amazing line of shale and limestone cliffs. The rocks in this area are Jurassic sedimentary with beds of shale, limestones, ironstones and sandstones, and in this picture we can see the rock looks remarkably crumbly and unstable. No climbers will be found on these cliffs. It is obvious that the coastline of north Yorkshire is constantly under threat of erosion by the North Sea.

BELOW Cleveland Way, Maw Wyke Hole, North Sea Coast *22 April*

After walking down through the caravan park at Hawsker Bottom, you finally get to see the cliffs of the North Sea at Maw Wyke Hole. There is a lovely sign post at the T-junction on the Cleveland Way, left to Whitby and right to your final destination, Robin Hood's Bay. Surrounded by bright yellow gorse on this warm, sunny afternoon in April, the blue sky and azure sea contrasted well. Whatever the weather, the spirits are lifted as it's not far to go now.

TOP LEFT Coastal path near Ness Point *22 April*

I looked back along my route on this lovely crisp, sunny day to see the gorse and blackthorn flank the coastal path, as it snaked away over the brow. The yellow, gold and white worked well with the deep blue backdrop of sea and sky. There is still no sight of Robin Hood's Bay, but round Ness Point it comes into view.

LEFT Robin Hood's Bay from Ness Point *22 April*

This is what everyone is eager, or maybe in some cases even sorry, to see – Robin Hood's Bay, their final destination and the end of a long journey across the north of England. A small gap cut in the hedge at Ness Point or North Cheek gives a sneaky view. I was careful not to stand too close to the edge with my tripod, seeing how unstable the cliffs appear to be. A final march on, with the view once again obscured, before the much deserved celebrations and refreshments.

ABOVE Robin Hood's Bay *21 April*

Here we are looking towards South Cheek, which juts out into the sea below Ravenscar. Also known as the Scars, this geologically interesting beach of harder limestone reefs underlying shale, is rich in fossils as well as in excellent rock pools.

Once called Bay Town, this fascinating little village with its steep alleyways, secret passages and jumble of houses perched in precarious places had a thriving fishing industry, and in the eighteenth century, was reportedly the busiest smuggling community on the Yorkshire coast. Hiding places, bolt holes and secret passages abound and it was said that a bale of silk could pass from the bottom of the village to the top without leaving the houses. It appears from sixteenth century Dutch sea charts that Robin Hood's Bay was once more important than neighbouring Whitby. Whether Robin Hood really did use this bay as a retreat from danger by keeping a small fleet of fishing boats here is unlikely, but its charms have attracted many visitors, replacing fishing with tourism as the main source of income.

FAR LEFT Tight corner at the bottom of King Street *22 April*

LEFT CENTRE The Bay Hotel and Wainwright's Bar: the end of the road *21 April*
Finally, before getting that celebratory drink and certificate, your toes must be dipped. I just hope the tide's in, your blisters are healed, and your knees are still strong enough to take the final steep descent down through the cobbled streets to the chilly waters of the North Sea.

LEFT Boats near the jetty *21 April*

Recommended reading

Lakeland Landscapes by Rob Talbot and Robin Whiteman (Phoenix Press, 1997)

A Coast to Coast Walk: A Pictorial Guide by Alfred Wainwright (Frances Lincoln, revised by Chris Jesty, 2003)

A Northern Coast to Coast Walk Terry Marsh (Cicerone Press, 2004)

Coast to Coast with Wainwright photographed by Derry Brabbs (Frances Lincoln, 2008)

Shadows of a Changing Land by Peter Freeman (Polecat Press, 2008)

Swaledale by Roly Smith, photographs by Mike Kipling (Frances Lincoln, 2008)

Nine Standards: Ancient Cairns or Modern Folly by Stephen Walker (Hayloft Publishing, 2008)

Coast to Coast: The Wainwright Route by Sandra Bardwell (Rucksack Readers, 2010)

The Coast to Coast Walk by Martin Wainwright (Aurum Press, 2010)

Coast to Coast – the original B&B accommodation guide by Doreen Whitehead (Butt House, Keld, Richmond DL11 6LJ) or see website: www. coasttocoastguides.co.uk

Websites

www.coast2coast.co.uk
The official Coast to Coast website

www.coasttocoastguides.co.uk
Useful for guides to the route

www. wildennerdale.co.uk
Wild Ennerdale Project

www.nmrs.co.uk
Northern Mine Research Society

www.bbc.co.uk/weather
Weather forecasts

www.lakedistrict.gov.uk
Lake District National Park

www.yorkshiredales.org.uk
Yorkshire Dales National Park

www.northyorkmoors.org.uk
North York Moors National Park

www.yha.org.uk
UK Youth Hostels Association

Tourist Information Centres

Egremont: 12, Main Street, Egremont, Cumbria CA22 2DW. Tel: 01946 820693

Seatoller: Seatoller Barn, Seatoller, Borrowdale, Keswick, Cumbria CA12 5XN. Tel: 01768 777294

Kirkby Stephen: Market Square, Kirkby Stephen, Cumbria CA17 4QN. Tel: 01768 371199

Richmond: Friary Gardens, Victoria Road, Richmond, North Yorkshire DL10 4AJ. Tel: 01748 850252

Northallerton: The Applegarth Car Park, Northallerton, North Yorkshire DL7 8LZ. Tel: 01609 776864

Danby Lodge: The Moors Centre, Danby Lodge, Lodge Lane, Whitby, North Yorkshire YO21 2NB. Tel: 01287 660654

Whitby: Langhorne Road, Whitby, North Yorkshire YO21 1YN. Tel: 01947 602674

Support services

There are several specialist companies which will carry your gear every day and drop it off at your next stopping point. They will also arrange dropping-off and picking-up points at the start and end of your walk, because the train service to St Bees is sporadic and there is no rail link to Robin Hood's Bay.

Leading suppliers of these services include:-
Coast to Coast Packhorse: Tel: 01768 342028.
    www.cumbria.com/packhorse
Sherpa Van: Tel: 0871 520 0124.
    www.sherpavan.com
Coast to Coast Holiday & Baggage Services:
    Tel: 01642 489173

Maps

Strip Maps
Strip maps are great as you don't have to carry so many. But they are not so good for navigation if you have to come off route, or want to explore a wider area.
Harveys Coast to Coast West (1:40,000)
Harveys Coast to Coast East (1:40,000)

Ordnance Survey maps
OL33: Wainwright's Coast to Coast Walk (St Bees Head to Keld) published with Michael Joseph (1:25,000)
OL34: Wainwright's Coast to Coast Walk (Keld to Robin Hood's Bay) published with Michael Joseph (1:25,000)

Note: Both these maps are now out of print and only available second hand, but are useful as they include extracts from Wainwright, a walker's distance checklist and the geology of the walk

Other OS Maps
Explorer (1:25,000) Maps
OL4: English Lakes North-western area
OL5: English Lakes North-eastern Area
OL19: Howgill Fells & Upper Eden Valley
OL30: Yorkshire Dales Northern & Central Areas
302: Northallerton & Thirsk
304: Darlington & Richmond
OL26: North York Moors Western Area
OL27: North York Moors Eastern Area

Landranger (1:50,000) Maps
89: West Cumbria
(covers St. Bees through to Greenup)
90: Penrith & Keswick
(covers Buttermere to Shap)
91: Appleby-in-Westmorland
92: Barnard Castle & Richmond
93: Middlesbrough
94: Whitby & Eskdale
99: Northallerton & Ripon
100: Malton & Pickering

Photographer's Notes

Practicalities
As mentioned in the introduction, I occasionally spent hours or even days in a single location waiting to catch the optimal lighting or weather conditions. Furthermore the necessity for planning and reconnaissance trips, in addition to the rapid changeability of the weather, meant that repeat visits to any particular site were the norm rather than the exception.

Wherever possible, I have used either side-lighting or back-lighting so that shadows and highlights are created which give more depth to the image. Although extremely time consuming, I'd rather start with the best image I can in the right light rather than try and fiddle a bad one in post-processing later. Fortunately some subjects, for example flowers or woodland, are better tackled on cloudy days when contrast is low and I could always find something to photograph whatever the weather. Occasionally, I would photograph in the rain to try and give some impression of the conditions that every Coast to Coaster must experience at some point on the trip. The front cover photo of Haweswater was taken when it was raining and with dusk fast approaching.

Use of a tripod

Preferably, I would always use a tripod with a self-timer on the camera. However, for some of the wilder locations where a long walk was necessary, I sometimes left my tripod behind and found other ways of reducing camera shake, particularly in low light or where I needed a slow shutter speed to record movement. This can be achieved by propping my camera on a beanbag or my rucksack. Failing that I would use my lightweight 'gorilla pod,' but this is always time-consuming and fiddly when compared with my usual sturdy tripod.

As a last resort, if faster shutter speeds were required when I had to hand-hold, I would use a higher ISO number to increase the sensitivity of the sensor just as a higher ISO for film does. The downside is a slight loss in quality as digital 'noise' can creep in above 800 ISO, depending on the camera make and model used.

Filters

I use a minimum of filters, mainly a polariser and a series of neutral density graduated (or grey grad) filters. Put simply, a polariser, when used at 90 degrees to the sun, cuts out surface reflections from foliage, resulting in more saturated colours and also has the effect of deepening blue skies. Neutral density graduated filters are used in order to even out the tonal differences in an image, such as a bright sky and dark foreground, for example. The human eye can cope with a much greater tonal range than a camera sensor or film.

Post-Processing

Personally, I hate spending time on computers and so try to do as little post-processing as possible. I use Adobe Photoshop and Lightroom 2 to make selective adjustments to contrast and brightness. I rarely need to adjust colour balance, hue and saturation if the picture has been taken correctly. Sometimes if the tonal range is too great for filters to correct, then I will take two RAW file exposures (using a tripod), one exposed for the dark areas, and one for the bright part of the image and then blend them in Photoshop to create what the eye saw. However, I find this is time-consuming and only two images in the book have been processed this way (the shot of the sunset over Marske on page 78–79 and the Wainstones on page 99).

Film and digital

A number of the older images were made on slide film which was subsequently scanned and digitised. Latterly, most of them were taken using digital Nikon SLR cameras with a variety of lenses. See the equipment list below.

EQUIPMENT
Cameras and lenses

Film Cameras

35mm Nikon F90 with the following lenses:
Nikon   17-35mm F4/5.6
Tokina 28-70 F2.8
Sigma 100-300mm F4
Nikon 105mm macro F2.8
Pentax 6 x7 with 105mm lens

Digital Cameras

Nikon D70 and D200 with use of the above 35mm
    film lenses plus:
Nikon 18-70mm F 3.5-4.5 G ED DX
Nikon D700 FX full frame digital with use of the
    above Nikon film lenses plus
Nikon 24-85mm F2.8-4 D

Tripods

Manfrotto 190ProB and O55CXPRO3 with a
    lightweight magnesium head and quick release
    plate attached to the camera.
Gorilla Pod
Bean bag

Film

Fuji Velvia 50 ISO transparency film for its superb fine grain and saturated colours, particularly on dull days.

Filters

Circular polariser in either a Cokin or Lee filter system with adapter rings so that you only need to buy one filter if you have different lenses of varying thread size. They also have slots for positioning other filters to be used together with this filter.

Neutral density graduated Lee 1 stop (0.3), 2 stop (0.6) and 3 stop (0.9) soft gradation filters

Accessories

Nikon Cable release, Jessops hot shoe spirit level, small Lastolite reflector.

Acknowledgements

Many thanks go to my friends and family who have been so patient and supportive throughout this project, and to all those people I met along the route who gave me useful tips and interesting information along the way.

I would also like to thank the following people:
Grace Farmer for her great help editing my first
    draft over a two-year period.
Graham and Jo Salisbury, Mathew, Sarah, Cathy
    and Becky Page, John and Jane Entwistle
    for their excellent hospitality, food and
    accommodation, often with very little warning.
Finally, my husband David for the hours of work he
    put in to help me finish this book, and for his
    willingness to drop everything and drive miles
    in order to join me, camping in all weathers
    when the conditions were right.

PRINTS

Archival prints and prints on canvas are available in any size for any of the images from this book. See www.karen frenkel.info for contact details and prices.

Index

Allen Crags 24
Angle Tarn 1
Arkengarthdale 76

Bay Town (Robin Hood's Bay) 106, 107, 108, 109
Bents Farm 48
Black Hill (Swaledale) 70
Black Sail 21
Blakey Moor 101
Bluebells 86
Bluebell Inn 91
Bolton on Swale 87
Boggle Hole (Swaledale) 58
Boredale 34
Borrowdale Valley 25
Bowness Knott 20
Buttermere Lake 22–23

Calver Hill 76
Carlton Bank 98
Carlton Moor 95, 96–97
Castle Crag 26
Cleveland Plain 96–97
Cleveland Way 96–97, 105
Codale Tarn 28
Colburn Beck 86
Cold Moor 98, 99
Comb Gill 24
Cotterby Scar 59
Crackpot Hall 64
Crosby Ravensworth Fell 40
Crummock Water 21

Dale Head 101
Danby High Moor 100
Danby Wiske 89
Deepdale 2-3, 8
Dent Fell 18
Drumlins 8
Dunmail Raise 30

Eagle Crag 26
East Applegarth 80
Eden Valley 51
East Gill Force 61
Fast Grain Smelt Mill 72
Ennerdale 7, 20, 21

Fair Head Lane 104
Falling Foss Waterfall 104
Faraday Gill 56
Far Easedale Gill 30
Far Jetticks 105
Farndale 101
Fat Betty 100
Field Barns (Swaledale) 66–67, 71

Fleetwith Pike 7, 22–23
Fleswick Bay 13,14
Forget-me-knots 86
Fremington Edge 76

Gamelands Stone Circle 43
Glaisedale Rigg 101
Glaramara 24
Grasmere Church 31
Grasmere Common 28
Grasmere Lake 31
Grassmoor 21
Great Fryup Dale 101
Great Gable 21
Great Tongue 31
Greenup Edge 26
Grinton 76
Grisedale 32
Grosmont Station 102-103
Gunnerside 71

Harkerside Moor 74-75
Harter Fell 35
Hartley 54-55
Hartley Fell 51
Hasty Bank 98, 99
Haweswater 34
Haweswater Beck 36
Hayeswater 35
Hay meadows (Swaledale) 67, 68–69
Helm Crag 29, 30
Helvellyn 32
Herdwick Sheep 27
High Stile 20
High Street 35
Holly Hill, Richmond 82–83
Honister 26
Homerell Hole 4–5
Howgills 41, 42
How Edge Scars 58

Ingleby Arncliffe 91
Ingleby Cross 91
Isle of Man 16–17

Keld, Shap 37
Keld, Swaledale 63, 66, 67
Kidsty Pike 35, 37
King Street, Robin Hood's Bay 108
Kiplin Hall 88
Kirkby Stephen 52-53
Kisdon Gorge 62
Kisdon Side 64-65
Kittiwakes 15
Knott Lane 43

Langstrath Beck 27

Lazenby Hall 89
Limekiln Hill 51
Limestone Pavements 40
Live Moor 95
Little Beck 104

Mallerstang Edge 48, 51
Mardale Green 34
Mardale Ill Bell 35
Marrick Priory 77
Martindale Common 1
Marske 78-79
Maw Wyke Hole 105
Measand 34
Moorland Crosses 100
Muker 64-65, 67, 70

Nannycatch 19
Ness Point 106
Nethermost Cove 32
Nine Standards Rigg 57
Northern Pennines 38–39
North Yorkshire Moors Railway 102–103

Oddendale Stone Circle 38–39
Old Gang Beck 73
Old Gang Smelt Mill 73
Orton Scar 41
Orton Village 41, 42
Osmotherley 93
Ovenmouth 59

Patterdale 2–3, 9
Pebbles 15
Pillar Ridge 7
Pillar Rock 20
Place Fell 32–33

Ravenscar 107
Ravenseat 58
Red Pike 20, 21
Reeth 74–75, 76
Reynoldson Syke 59
Richmond 80-81, 82-83, 84, 85
Riggindale 35
River Swale 60, 61, 62, 64-65, 74-75, 80, 85
Robin Hood's Bay 106, 107, 108, 109
Roseberry Topping 95
Rosedale Head 100
Rosedale Ironstone Railway 101
Rosthwaite 25
Rough Crag 35
Rowantreethwaite Beck 36

Satura Crag 1
Scandal Beck 49, 50

Scarry Wood 104
Scurvy Grass 15
Seathwaite 24
Seatoller 24
Sellafield 12
Sergeant Man 28
Several's Settlement 49
Shap Abbey 37
Shore Platforms 4–5
Smardale 49, 50
Smardale Fell 51
Smardale Gill 49, 50
Smardale Viaduct 49, 50
Smithymire Island 27
Sour Milk Gill 30
South Cheek 107
South Wood 92
Squeezer stiles 68
Station Bridge, Richmond 85
St. Bees 10–11, 13
St. Bees Head 13
Stonethwaite Beck 27
Stonethwaite Valley 26–27
Straights of Riggindale 35
Streetlam 88
Street Lane, Orton 42
Striding Edge 32
St. Sunday Crag 32–33
Sunbiggin Tarn 44–45, 46–47
Surrender Mill 73
Swinner Gill 72
Sydal Lodge 91

Tailbridge 51
The Hermitage 104
The Howitzer 30
The Rigg 34
Thorneythwaite Fell 24
Thornthwaite Force 36
Tongue Gill 31
Trough House 100

Uldale 19
Ullswater 6, 32
Upper Lune Valley 41

Vale of Mowbray 80-81
Wain Stones 98, 99
Wain Wath Force 60
Wainwright's Bar 108
Whitcliffe Scar 80
Whiteless Pike 21
Whitsundale Beck 58, 59
Wood Anemone 104
Wood Howe 34

Young Ralph Cross 100

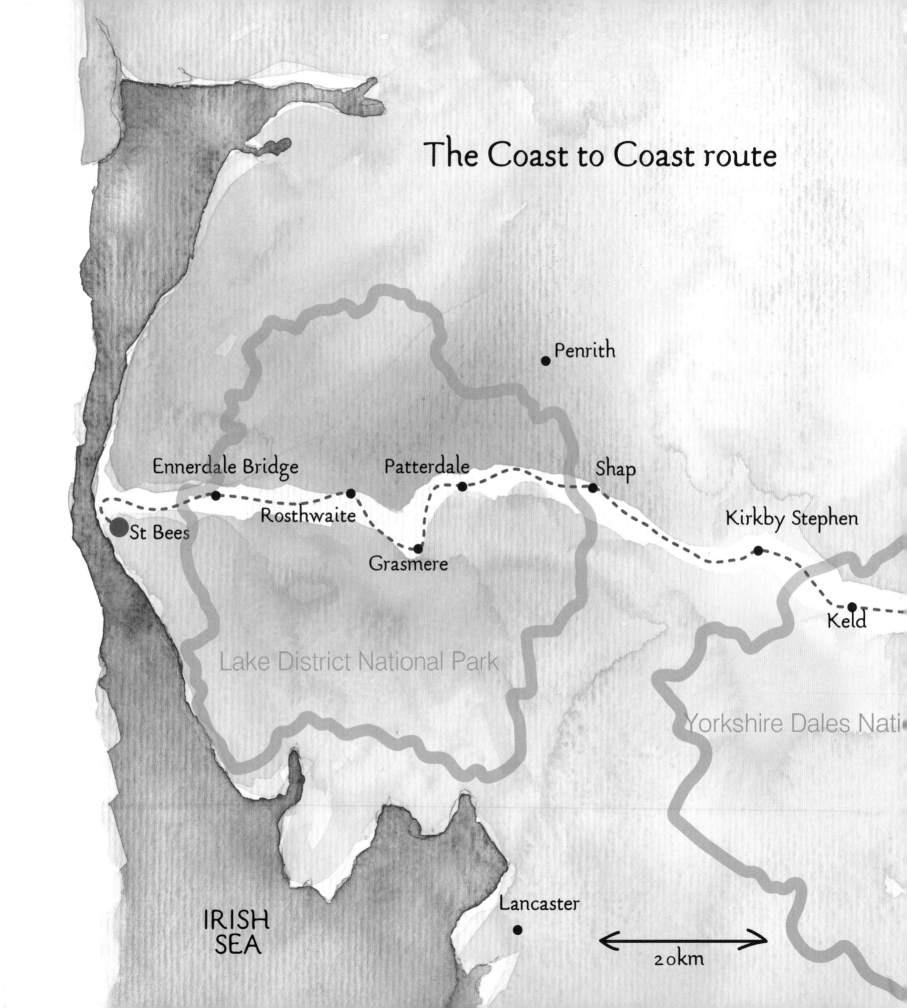

The Coast to Coast route

Penrith

Ennerdale Bridge

Patterdale

Shap

Rosthwaite

Kirkby Stephen

St Bees

Grasmere

Keld

Lake District National Park

Yorkshire Dales Nati

IRISH
SEA

Lancaster

20km